A JOURNEY THROUGH ISLAMIC HISTORY

A SHORT TIMELINE OF KEY EVENTS

Yasminah Hashim
Muhammad Beg

First published in England by Kube Publishing Ltd,
Markfield Conference Centre
Ratby Lane, Markfield,
Leicestershire LE67 9SY
United Kingdom
Tel: +44 (0) 1530 249230
Fax: +44 (0) 1530 249656
Website: www.kubepublishing.com
Email: info@kubepublishing.com

© Yasminah Hashim and Muhammad Beg, 2012
All rights reserved

The right of Yasminah Hashim and Muhammad Beg
to be identified as the authors of this work has been
asserted by them in accordance with the
Copyright, Designs and Patents Act, 1988.

Cataloguing-in-Publication Data is available from the British Library

ISBN 978-1-84774-028-1 casebound

Design, Typesetting and Layout: Bayan Naseer and Zain Jamjoom

CONTENTS

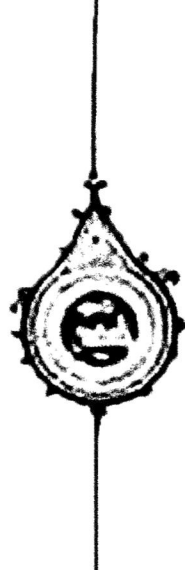

v.	**FOREWORD** By Professor Salim T. S. Al-Hassani
vi.	**INTRODUCTION** By Yasminah Hashim
1-16	**THE PROPHET MUHAMMAD** 570-632 CE/54 BH-11 AH
17-26	**THE RIGHTLY-GUIDED CALIPHS** 632-661 CE/11-41 AH
27-36	**THE UMAYYADS** 661-750 CE/41-132 AH
37-70	**THE 'ABBASIDS** 750-1258 CE/132-656 AH
71-82	**THE MAMLUKS** 1250-1517 CE/648-923 AH
83-106	**THE OTTOMANS, SAFAVIDS AND MUGHALS** 1501-1924 CE/906-1342 AH
107-114	**THE RISE OF EUROPEAN POWER** 1800-1924 CE/ 1214-1342 AH
115-129	**THE MODERN MUSLIM NATION-STATES** 1924-2011 CE/1342-1432 AH
131-132	SHORT GLOSSARY
133-135	INDEX
136	PICTURE CREDITS

FOREWORD

This work brings together much needed material on Islamic history and Muslim heritage. The book interweaves numerous events of historical importance in an interesting timeline. The selection of events and people has been cleverly done to enable the reader to pick out role models for the next generation. Amongst other interesting aspects, it also alludes to numerous contributions in science and culture made during the golden age of Muslim civilisation.

The world today needs to invest a great deal in reviving the spirit of harmony between various faiths amongst the scholars and scientists which prevailed during the golden centuries of Muslim civilisation, commonly and wrongly known as the Dark or Medieval Ages. We can learn great lessons from the golden centuries of Muslim civilisation to inspire future generations and to engender understanding and respect amongst the various cultures and nations. One effective means to achieve this is to undertake research and then to popularise the cultural roots of science and invention.

This subject has commonly been neglected by school curricula worldwide; however, it is now becoming increasingly recognised as an important area for support and recognition. This book helps to raise awareness of the scientific legacy of the men and women from that period.

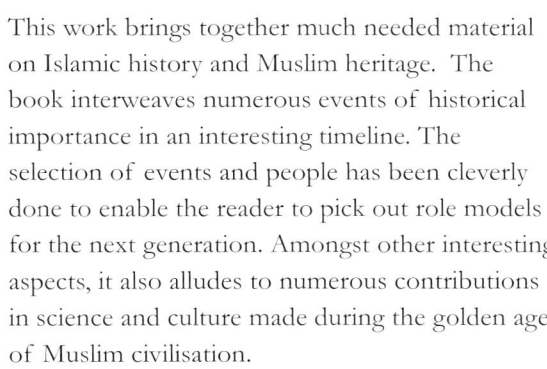

Considering that Yasminah Hashim is a final year undergraduate student, this work is a remarkable achievement. Yasminah is an intelligent and rigorous writer who has written this book under the guidance of the able historian, Dr Muhammad A. J. Beg. They have applied themselves to the creation of this book with great dedication and enthusiasm.

PROFESSOR
SALIM T. S. AL-HASSANI

CHAIRMAN, FOUNDATION FOR SCIENCE,
TECHNOLOGY AND CIVILISATION
MAY 2011

مقدمه INTRODUCTION

Transforming a brutal society into the most advanced nation in the world in two generations. Pioneering university education. Installing the first free public hospital. Introducing street lighting and establishing peace in whichever province they conquered. Do you know what all these varied achievements have in common? They have all been products of one civilisation – the classical Islamic civilisation.

The history of Islam is one of the greatest and richest histories of all time. When you read of the history of Muslims and examine how rapidly they became one of the world's leading nations, you would think at first that it was a miracle. But in fact it was their strong allegiance to Islam, a religion that encouraged them to seek knowledge, along with their determination and faith in their Creator and their sense of duty, that made this miracle possible.

At a time when Islamic culture is the subject of growing interest, this book offers a glimpse of that history, a past that is considered an achievement for its age, and one that deserves to be brought back to life, fully understood and fairly judged.

Believing strongly in the value of history in general and, in particular, of Islamic history, I present this research in hope that it will be a stimulating and exciting introduction. *A Journey through Islamic History* introduces a sweep of Islamic history, beginning with the birth of the Prophet Muhammad and concluding with the year 2010. It includes a selection of the important political and cultural events in the history of Islam, arranged in the form of a timeline. This book acts as an aid in connecting the dots of Islamic history, and is meant to be precise rather than comprehensive. For further details, the interested reader may consult the essays and textboxes that outline the overall story and context.

Although this book focuses more on the political aspects of Islamic history due to limitations of space, it should be noted that there is more to history than politics. Cultural, social and economic history is of great value too, and it is reflected in the book too. The ideas and values people hold, and the economic and social systems they are part of, as well as the scientific and intellectual advances they made offer all of us a deep insight into the real lives of the people of the era. History in all its forms cannot go unappreciated: providing a rounded depiction of our past human experience allows us to reflect more fully upon our present condition.

In this field only one thing holds greater importance than history itself: the philosophy of history, which is the attempt to not only understand the facts, but to go beyond them. It is to move beyond simple facts to analyse and give history some shape and sense with the aim of extracting those lessons that would help us to overcome the problems of today and to shape with more wisdom the patterns of tomorrow. *A Journey through Islamic History* offers a glimpse of the facts, and I hope it will encourage you to continue to be curious, to question and to pursue your own answers.

I would like to acknowledge all those who have helped me to put this book together. I owe special gratitude to Dr. Tariq al-Suwaidan and Mr Amr Khaled for making me determined to make a difference, Dr Muhammad Beg who wrote the essays that accompany the chronology, the late Dr Kadhem al-Rawi and Dr Salim Ayduz who guided me through the research, and Dr Manazir Ahsan for his guidance and generous advice.

I would also like to thank my two loving parents for encouraging me and believing in me; Mrs. Jeani Baker and Dr. Tom Alibrandi for grammatical assistance; my aunt Awatif Baarma and my cousins and friends Suhaila and Salwa Baarma; Mounia al-Darwish and Dalia Bin-Mahfouz who shared knowledge and inspiration with me; my cousins and friends Mariam and Jumana Binmahfouz, Rania Jamjoom, Sara Mohannah and Bayan Naseer for their creative artistic ideas; and last but not least my brothers and sisters, my friends Layla Al-Nahdi, Dina Naghi, Shahd Alghamdi and Lina Binladin for their encouragement and enthusiasm.

Finally I would like to dedicate this book to my beloved uncle, Muhammad Baarma, a great admirer of history, who never had the chance to create a similar project many years ago, 'may Allah have mercy on him'.

YASMINAH HASHIM
JANUARY 2011
JEDDAH

The Prophet Muhammad

54BH-11AH
570-632 CE

Some historians have rightly claimed that Islam, unlike Judaism or Christianity, emerged in the full light of recorded history. The Prophet Muhammad's first divine revelation (*wahy* or *tanzil*) can be traced to a time and a place recorded by scholars: to the year 610 in a cave of Mount Hira', just outside the city of Makkah. The Prophet received revelation over a period of 23 years, and the final revelation was given at the plain of 'Arafat in 632.

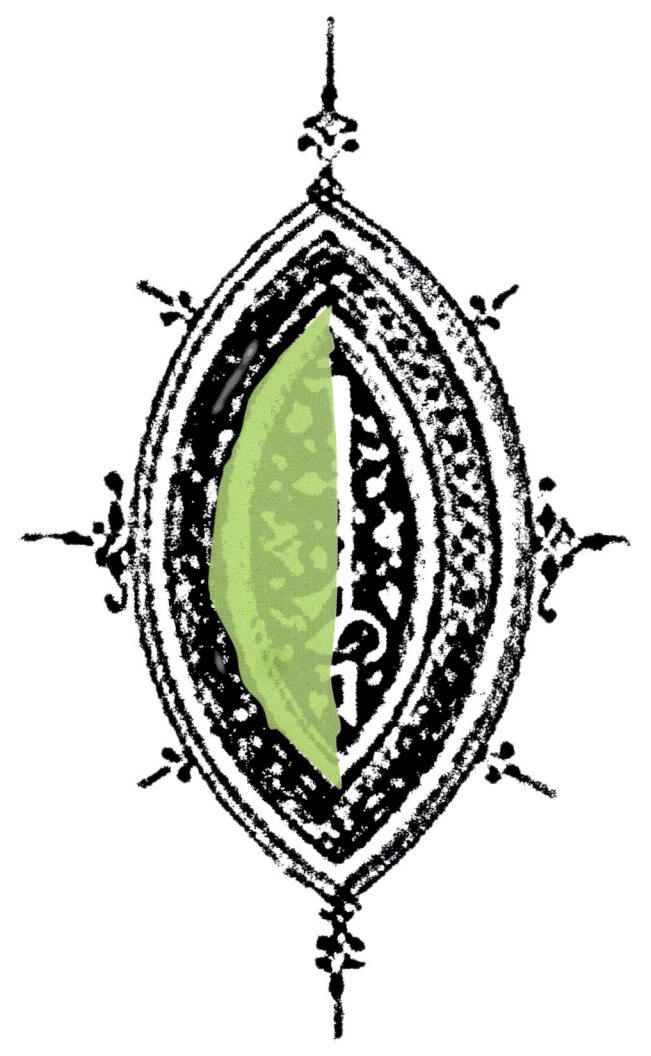

Mount Hira'

The entrance to the cave on Mount Hira', where the Prophet received the first revelations in 610

The rise of Islam was recorded by the first biographers of the Prophet Muhammad, such as Muhammad ibn Ishaq and Ibn Hisham. Unlike other prophets before him, the Prophet not only established a new community (*ummah*) but also founded the city-state of Madinah which was governed by a written constitution (*sahifah*). The Prophet Muhammad was both its spiritual guide and its head of state. He led its citizens both in war and peace, maintaining law and order, defending the community against its enemies on the battlefield and maintaining diplomatic contact with foreign powers, such as the Negus (al-Najashi) of Abyssinia (Ethiopia), Heraclius, the Emperor of the Byzantine (or Eastern Roman) Empire in Constantinople, and Khusraw Parviz, the Shahanshah of Sasanian Persia. He also sent diplomatic letters to Arab tribal chiefs of Yamamah, Ghassan, Oman, Dawmat al-Jandal, Ma'an, Bahrain, Himyar, the Yemen and Hadramawt.

The basic work of the Prophet was his mission (*da'wah*), based on the message of the Qur'an and his own inspired example and teaching to his disciples or Companions. His preaching (*da'wah*) involved teaching the Qur'an to new converts, and affirming that there was no deity except Allah and that Muhammad (may Allah bless him and grant him peace) was the servant and Messenger of God (*see page 6*). Acceptance of this basic message of Islam had practical consequences for the converts. The new Muslims consciously rejected polytheism (*shirk*) and their devotion was only to Allah and the emulation of the Prophet in individual and collective worship. The followers of monotheism (*tawhid*) constituted a new community (*ummah*) in Makkah.

The Companions of the Prophet began to encounter opposition from those who maintained their old way of life and the worship of ancestral gods (*al-taghut*) housed inside and outside the Ka'bah, the holy sanctuary at Makkah, that had been originally built by Abraham for the one true God (*see page 10*). The polytheists resisted the

Prophet's invitation to Islam and showed hostility to him in various ways. Despite their opposition, however, the number of Muslims continued to grow and the pagans then resorted to persecuting the new converts. As a result, the Prophet suggested that Muslims migrate to the Christian kingdom of Abyssinia (c.615-616) and wrote a letter to the emperor Negus as an act of diplomacy. This first migration resulted in the spread of Islam to the Horn of Africa. Later, Islam spread to other parts of Africa when the Prophet sent an envoy with a letter (c.628-629) inviting Muqawqis, the Prefect of Alexandria and Egypt, to embrace Islam. The Prophet also sent an envoy, Dihya ibn Khalifah, to the emperor Heraclius in Constantinople inviting him to Islam. He also sent an envoy to the court of the King of Kings (Shahanshah) of the Sasanian Empire of Persia, inviting him to convert. The Prophet strongly believed in the Qur'anic message of inviting people to Islam with wisdom and diplomacy; his preaching (da'wah) was thus full of wisdom.

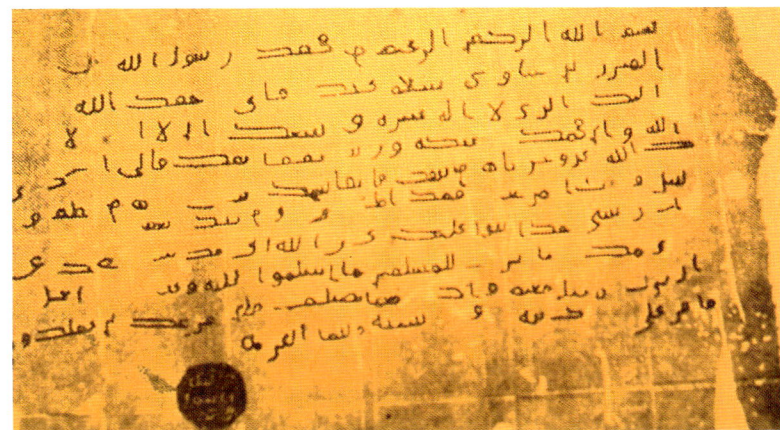

The Prophet's letter

To the ruler of Bahrain Munzir ibn Sawa al-Tamimi inviting him to Islam

The Prophet's Conquests and Missions, 623-632

THE PROPHET MUHAMMAD

Birth of the Prophet
Muhammad in Makkah

570CE 54BH

The Prophet is put in his uncle's
care after his grandfather's death

578CE 45BH

576CE 47BH

c.591–592CE c.32–33BH

Death of the
Prophet's mother

The Prophet forms the
Pact of the Virtuous

Silver Dirham

Silver dirham showing a
bust of King Khusraw
II of Persia, r. 590-627

While Islam spread through the peaceful missionary work of the Prophet and his dedicated disciples, the early Muslims, equipped with the knowledge of the Qur'an, united themselves under the guidance of the Prophet to face internal and external threats. His firm policy of defence of the community against the provocative actions of his opponents resulted in armed confrontations that culminated in the battles of Badr, Uhud, Khandaq, Khaybar, Mu'tah, Hunayn and Tabuk. The Prophet's intent to bring peace to Arabia led to the treaty of al-Hudaybiyah in 628, allowing for the peaceful performance of the greater pilgrimage (Hajj) to the Ka'bah the following year. In a clever move to end polytheism in Arabia, the Prophet led 10,000 of his disciples and allies on a campaign to Makkah, achieving its peaceful surrender in 630. The Ka'bah was cleansed of its false idols, and the Prophet proclaimed God's

The Prophet marries Khadijah bint Kuwaylid

595CE 28BH

message of the advent of the truth and the departure of falsehood. Thus Islam triumphed over traditional Arabian polytheism. The process of divine revelation that had began in the month of Ramadan in 610 came to completion in 632 when, in the midst of the Farewell pilgrimage, the Prophet received at 'Arafat the final revelation from Allah proclaiming the perfection of Islam.

In the early years of revelation, the command to perform ablution and the prayer at the Ka'bah came even before many converts had been won. The Prophet and his wife Khadijah (*see page 14*) started praying at the Ka'bah to the shock and amazement of the pagan spectators. Later, in 621, in the company of Gabriel (Jibril), the Prophet ascended to Heaven on a heavenly mount called Buraq, where he stood before his Creator. Then, during the Ascension (Mi'raj), Allah made the ritual five daily prayers compulsory for the Muslims. Prayer (*salah*), which is the second pillar of Islam and a hallmark of Islam to this day, was established at Makkah, shortly before the Prophet's migration (*hijrah*) to Madinah in 622.

The Rock inside the Dome of the Rock

In Jerusalem, from where tradition records that the Prophet ascended to Heaven in 621

WHAT IS ISLAM?

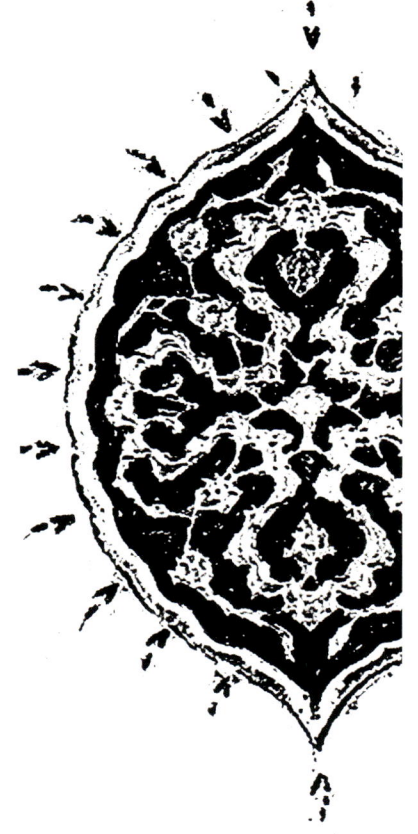

From its Arabic root, Islam means surrender to God through which peace may be attained, by following faithfully the ethical way of life revealed by God through His Prophet Muhammad. So Islam is the name of religion in its fullest sense, referring to the covenant between humanity and God that humankind freely recognises and worships God and lives the good life in accordance with what God has ordained. This same fundamental message was revealed to all peoples of the world through prophets and messengers that were sent to them, and whose universal message was completed by the last Prophet of God, Muhammad, who was sent to all peoples as a 'mercy unto the worlds'. The distinguishing feature of Islam is its primary insistence upon the truth that there is no deity worthy of adoration and worship except for the One True God, Who has no partners or offspring, Who created the entirety of creation and to Whom all humanity will eventually return after death to be judged for its conduct on earth.

The Kalimah

The Kalimah, 'I bear witness that there is no deity except God', traditional Turkish tile

Besides the declaration of faith in one God and the final prophethood of Muhammad, the foundations of Islam are also built upon the observance of the regular five daily prayers, giving in charity to the poor, fasting during the month of Ramadan and performing the Greater Pilgrimage or Hajj to Makkah.

Built upon these foundations of belief and practice are a holistic set of Islamic principles that shape economics, politics, and social behaviour. The broadness of these principles allows plenty of scope for changes in application that is required to keep Islamic principles relevant in all times and ages.

610CE 13BH
The Prophet receives the first revelations of the Qur'an

On his arrival at the outskirts of Madinah, the Messenger of Allah led and performed the first congregational prayer (*salat al-jumu'ah*) and delivered the first Friday sermon (*khutbah*) at Quba, where a mosque was later built. Thus a new phase of Islam was begun at Madinah. Whereas in Makkah the Muslims were a persecuted community that sometimes had to perform the group prayer in a valley outside the city, in Madinah they had the opportunity to perform without persecution under the leadership (*imamah*) of the Messenger of Allah. Indeed the Islamic calendar itself starts with the migration of the Prophet to Madinah, and, in a way, marks too the very idea of Islamic history itself. 'History' is described by the Arabic term '*ta'rikh*', which also means 'chronology'.

In 624, the direction of prayer (*qiblah*) was changed from Jerusalem (Bayt al-Maqdis) to the Ka'bah in Makkah. In the same year, fasting in the month of Ramadan (*sawm*) was made compulsory for Muslims. While the Muslims were fasting on the seventeenth day of Ramadan, they fought against the Quraysh, and won a decisive victory at Badr. The institution of the greater pilgrimage (Hajj) was made compulsory for Muslims in

613CE 10BH
The Prophet first preaches Islam in Makkah

615CE 8BH
Persecution of Muslims in Makkah; some seek refuge in Abyssinia

628, when the noble Prophet, accompanied by 3000 of his Companions, prepared to travel to Makkah as pilgrims. The pilgrims were thwarted by the Quraysh at Hudaybiyah, but a truce was agreed between the two parties that brought peace to Arabia for a decade. After the signing of the truce (*hudnah*), the Prophet sacrificed camels to celebrate the 'Id al-Adha. In the following year, the Prophet's close friend, Abu Bakr, led the Companions (Sahabah) on the first formal pilgrimage to Makkah.

The Prophet urged Muslims to give charity (*sadaqah*). It is not precisely known when obligatory charity (*zakat*) was instituted in Islam, but it is certain that in the Year of the Delegations (*'am al-wufud*) in 631 that the Prophet appointed *Zakat* collectors and sent them to various Arabian tribes.

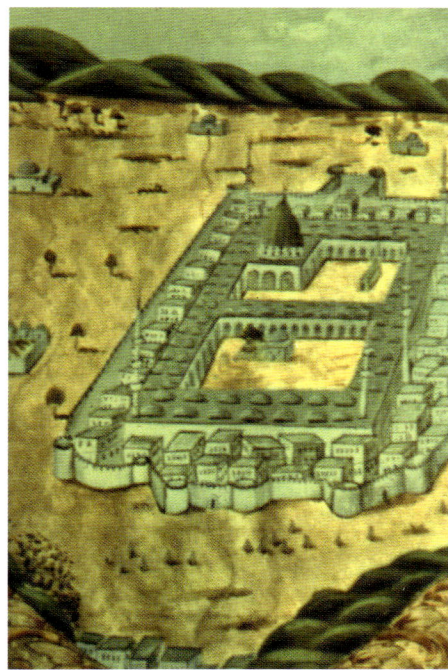

The Prophet's Mosque

The Prophet's Mosque in the city of Madinah during the Ottoman period

LIFE IN ARABIA BEFORE ISLAM

Polytheism and the worship of idols were common among the Arabs before Islam. Idols were kept in some houses, and the ancient sanctuary in Makkah, the Ka'bah, was surrounded by 360 idols. However monotheism was not unknown to the Arabs either: some Jewish tribes had settled in the Hijaz in western Arabia, and Judaism had spread to certain parts of the Yemen in southern Arabia as well. Christianity was known among the southern and northern Arab tribes, and Zoroastrianism had a presence too in those parts of eastern Arabia close to the Sasanid Empire.

Even if there was clannish and tribal solidarity to be found among the sedentary Arabs, inter-tribal conflict was ever-present. However, attempts were made to forge alliances among certain tribes to limit conflict, and the Arabs generally upheld the sacredness of the four months in which war was forbidden.

Trade was the primary source of income amongst the Arabs, yet due to the instability of political life and continuous tribal war, it only really flourished during the four-month truce. As a result, poverty and hunger remained a common feature in most parts of society.

Adultery was commonplace, as well as multiple marriages, among both men and women. Men were generally seen as superior to women, and boys were preferred to girls. Female infanticide was carried out by the brutal act of burying infant girls alive out of the superstitious belief that a daughter would bring shame upon the family.

Yet although such corruption was widespread in Arabia, the virtues of keeping promises, courage, integrity, pride, generosity, and hospitality were widely upheld and practised among the Arabs. They were noted too for their eloquence and love of poetry.

Arabia before the advent of Islam the Prophet seemed ripe for reform and transformation from the conveyor of a universal message from God, a great spiritual guide, social reformer and unifying political leader, whom the Arabs of the day had few inklings would come to change them forever.

Old pre-Islamic Arabian rock inscription

> **ALL MANKIND** IS FROM ADAM AND EVE: AN ARAB HAS NO SUPERIORITY OVER A NON-ARAB NOR A NON-ARAB HAS ANY SUPERIORITY OVER AN ARAB; ALSO A WHITE MAN HAS NO SUPERIORITY OVER A BLACK MAN NOR DOES A BLACK MAN HAVE ANY SUPERIORITY OVER A WHITE MAN EXCEPT BY PIETY AND GOOD ACTION. LEARN THAT EVERY MUSLIM IS A BROTHER TO EVERY MUSLIM AND THAT THE MUSLIMS CONSTITUTE ONE BROTHERHOOD.

Extract from the Farewell Sermon of the Prophet

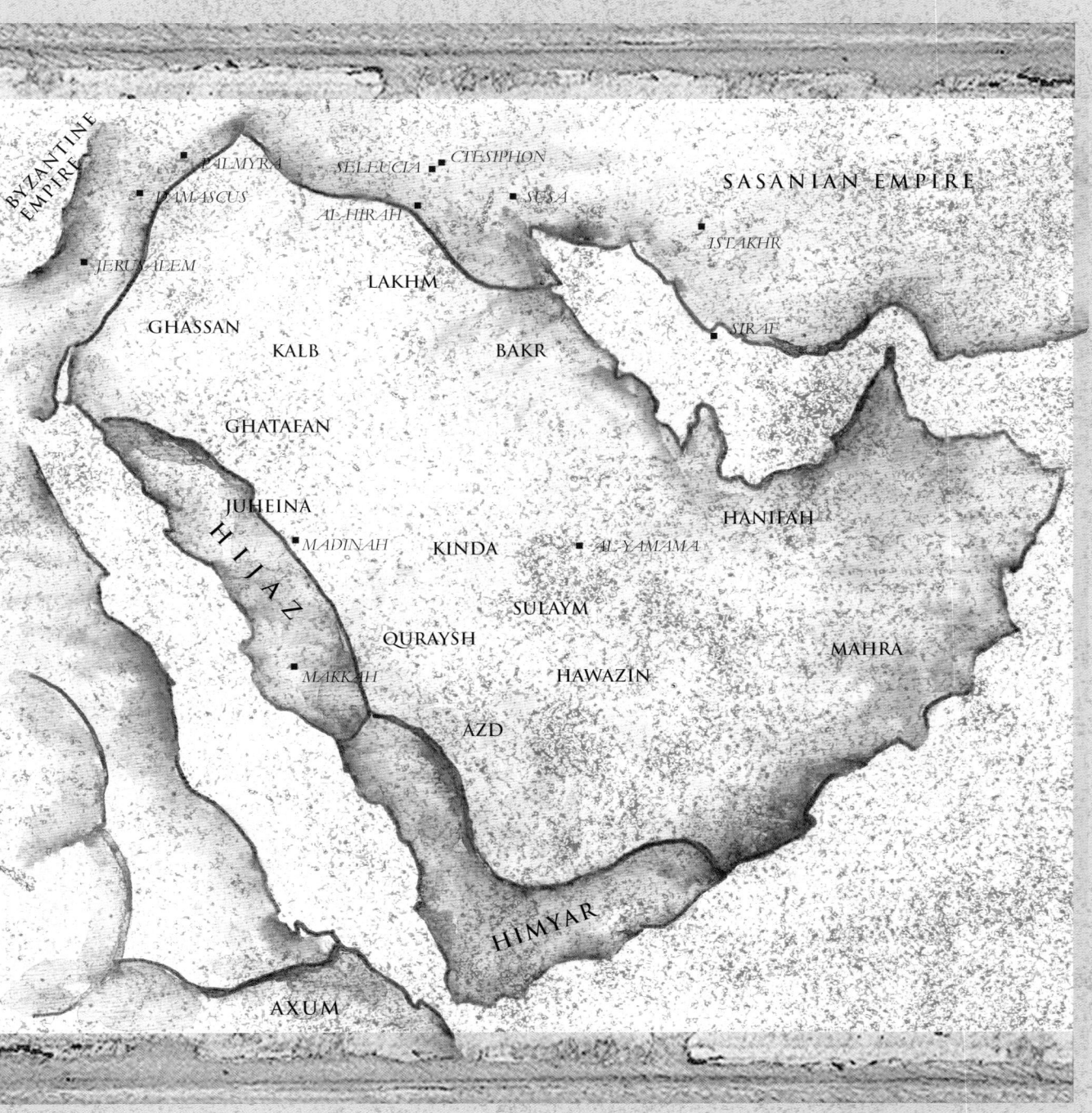

Pre-Islamic Empires and Tribes

The main pre-Islamic Empires of the Middle East, plus the major tribes of the Arabian Peninsula

THE PROPHET MUHAMMAD

622CE 0AH

The Prophet's Migration to Madinah

The Ka'bah in Makkah

A traditional representation of the Ka'bah and the Grand Mosque in Makkah

During his farewell Pilgrimage in 632, the Prophet announced that he was leaving two fundamental sources for the guidance of the community: the Qur'an and the Sunnah (the Prophetic Tradition), which would provide guidance for its welfare in this world and the Hereafter. The Prophet made it a duty upon all Muslims to propagate the message of Islam to others. Integral to the way of the Prophet was the Islamic state, which was founded to implement the law and to defend the community from its enemies. The Islamic state was an existential necessity for the community to preserve Islam and its institutions.

After the Prophet completed his mission (*da'wah*) and trained his Companions to live an Islamic way of life, he became severely ill with fever and died on the 8th June, 632, at the age of 63. The community mourned his death but remained resolute in following the ideals of Islam under a new leader who was given the title of Successor to the Prophet, or *Khalifat Rasulullah*.

The death of the Prophet brought a profound crisis for the community. It has been suggested that it was like a constitutional crisis in a modern state or republic, but this comparison is an understatement. He was not a mere head of state but above all a Messenger of God (*Rasulullah*) who has no parallel in history. As God's Messenger and head of state, the most important activity of the Prophet was the propagation of the message of Islam to the Arabian tribes as well as to the foreign powers bordering Arabia. The spiritual and temporal activities of the Prophet laid down the very foundations of Islamic history.

630CE 8AH
The Muslim conquest of Makkah

632CE 10-11AH
The completion of revelation and the Prophet's death

The Battle of Badr, 623

THE PROPHET MUHAMMAD

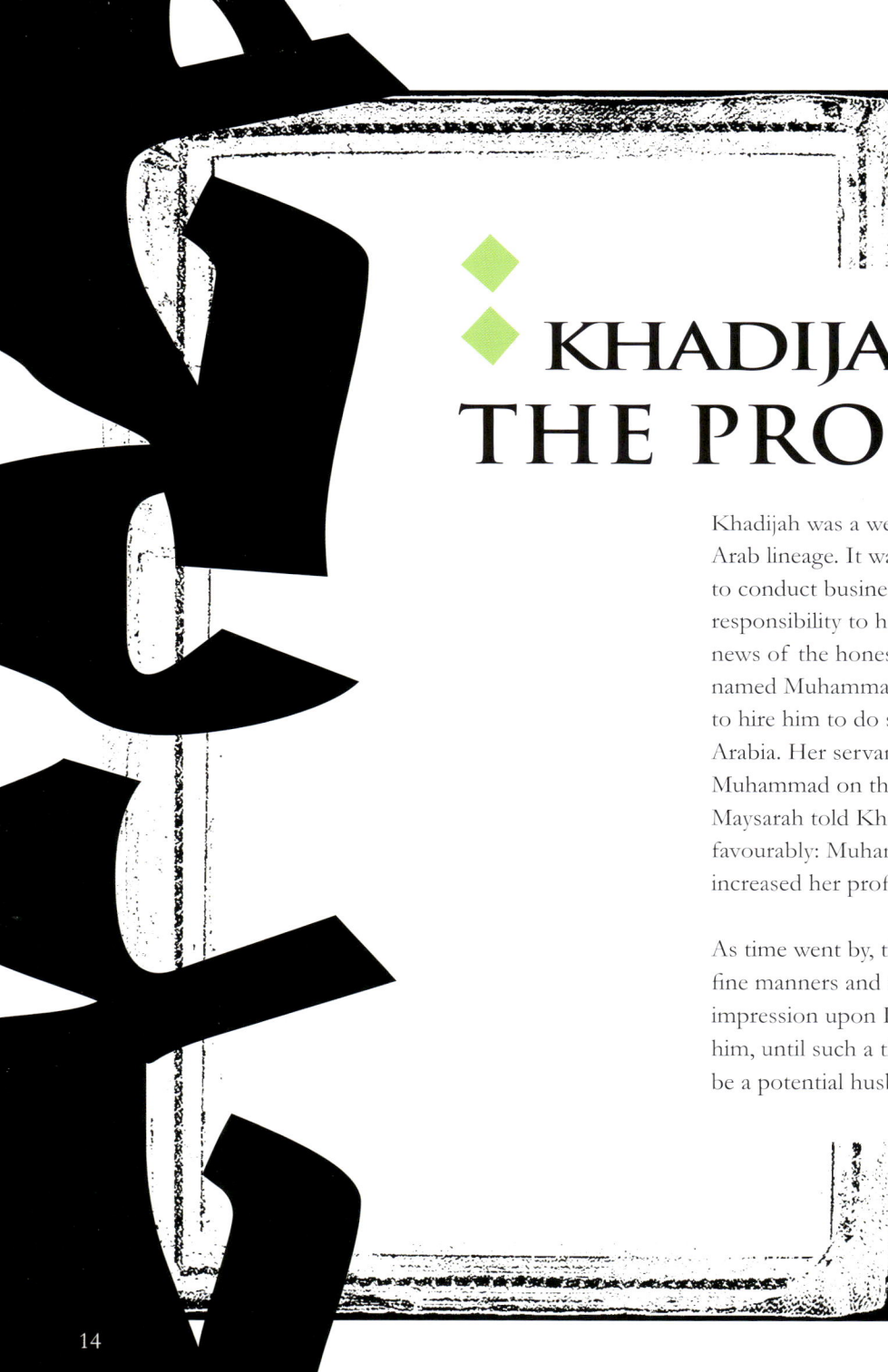

KHADIJAH BINT KHUWAYLID
THE PROPHET'S FIRST WIFE

Khadijah was a wealthy businesswoman of noble Arab lineage. It was her practice to hire men to conduct business on her behalf, giving them responsibility to handle her trading caravans. When news of the honesty and probity of a young man named Muhammad reached Khadijah, she decided to hire him to do some business for her in northern Arabia. Her servant Maysarah accompanied Muhammad on the trip, and upon their return, Maysarah told Khadijah that the trip had gone favourably: Muhammad's trading acumen had increased her profits.

As time went by, this young man's honesty, intellect, fine manners and sincerity, made a favourable impression upon Khadijah and she grew fond of him, until such a time that she considered him to be a potential husband. As a wealthy noblewoman, she always had many rich and eminent suitors, but she had refused them all. Khadijah confessed her thoughts to her friend Nufaysah, who then went to Muhammad and suggested that he propose to Khadijah, and he agreed to do so.

In 595, Muhammad and Khadijah got married; she was 40, and he was only 25. Khadijah was the first to accept Muhammad's prophethood and so became the first Muslim. She remained unwavering and staunch in her support throughout his years of trial in Makkah, spending all her wealth in aid of the early Muslims, and was forever after his most beloved wife. She bore him six children: al-Qasim, Zaynab, Ruqayyah, Umm Kulthum, Fatimah, and 'Abdullah. When Khadijah died in 619, the year of her death became known as the Year of Sorrow.

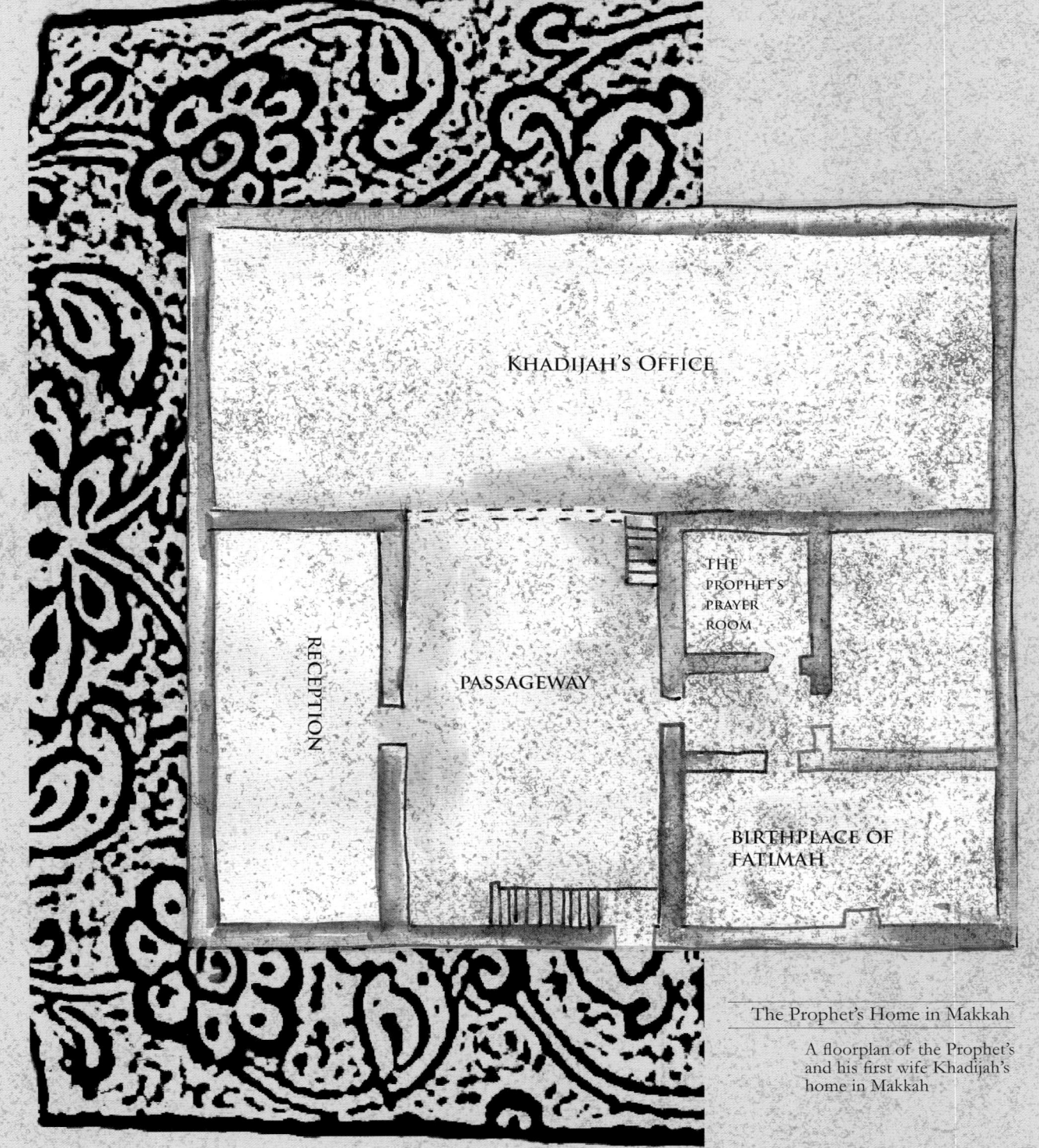

The Prophet's Home in Makkah

A floorplan of the Prophet's and his first wife Khadijah's home in Makkah

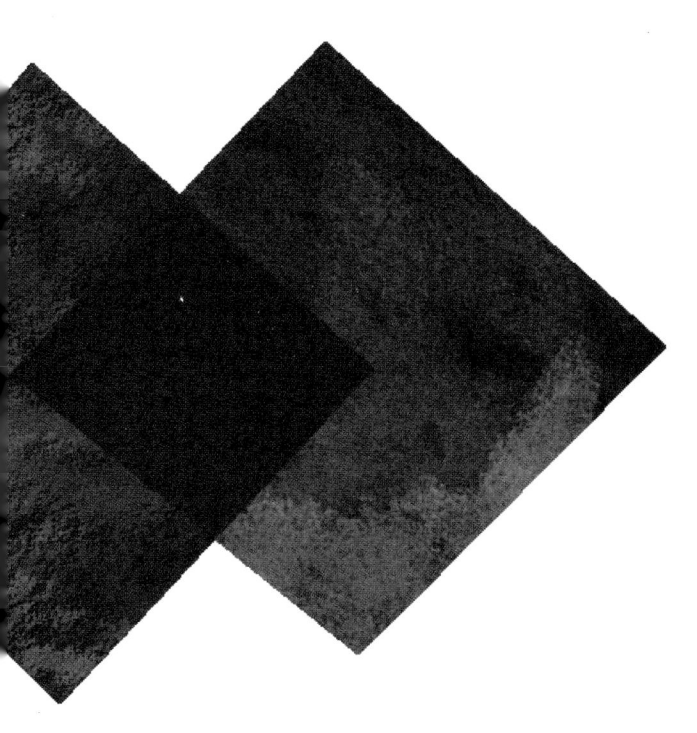

TIMELINE
THE PROPHET MUHAMMAD

FIRST CENTURY BH
SIXTH CENTURY CE

570 CE
54 BH
Birth of Muhammad ibn Abdullah in Makkah on 4th May (12 Rabi' al-Awwal). Orphaned at a young age, he is taken in by his grandfather 'Abd al-Muttalib.

575 CE
48 BH
The Sasanian army of Persia invades the Yemen and defeats the Abyssinians, bringing *de facto* Persian rule over South Arabia.

576 CE
47 BH
Death of Aminah bint Wahab, Muhammad's mother.

578 CE
45 BH
Death of 'Abd al-Muttalib, Muhammad's grandfather. Muhammad is put in the care of his uncle Abu Talib.

c.591 / 592 CE
c.32 / 33 BH
The formation of the Pact of the Virtuous (*Hilf al-Fudul*), involving Muhammad, that aimed to implement justice in Makkan society.

595 CE
28 BH
Muhammad marries Khadijah bint Khuwaylid.

605 CE
18 BH
The Quraysh reconstruct the Abrahamic holy site, the Ka'bah; Muhammad is asked to place the Black Stone (*Hajar al-Aswad*) to complete the reconstruction.

610 CE
13 BH
- Heraclius ascends to the throne of the Byzantine Empire in Constantinople.
- The Archangel Gabriel reveals the first verses of the Qur'an to Muhammad.
- Six months after the first revelation, Gabriel reveals to Muhammad that he is the Messenger of God.

613 CE
10 BH
The first public invitation to Islam at the hillock of Safa, after three years of private invitation (*see page 6*).

615 CE
8 BH
Persecution of Muslims by the polytheists of Makkah. The Prophet orders a group of Muslims to migrate to Abyssinia, where they are given refuge by the Christian king, al-Najashi.

617 CE
6 BH
A three-year boycott of the Prophet's tribe, the Hashimites, by the Quraysh begins, during which they face starvation.

619 CE
3 BH
Lifting of the Boycott. The deaths of Abu Talib and Khadijah, the Prophet's first wife (*see page 14*).

620 CE
2 BH
The Prophet's trip to Ta'if, where his call to Islam is rejected.

FIRST CENTURY AH
SEVENTH CENTURY CE

621 CE / 1 BH
- The Prophet's Night Journey to Jerusalem (*Al-Isra'*) and his Ascension to Heaven (*Al-Mi'raj*) and the granting of the five daily prayers (*salawat al-khamsah*).
- The First Pledge of 'Aqabah. Twelve men from Madinah pledge their obedience to the Prophet and promise to worship God alone, not to steal, commit adultery or practise customary infanticide.

622 CE / 0 AH
- The Second Pledge of 'Aqabah. Seventy-three men and two women pledge their obedience, protection and support to the Prophet.
- The Migration of the Prophet from Makkah to Yathrib, renamed Madinah, which also marks the beginning of the Islamic or Hijri calendar.

622–623 CE / 1 AH
- The building of the Prophet's Mosque in Madinah.
- The promulgation of the Constitution (*Sahifah*) of Madinah, in which the Prophet grants the Muslims and non-Muslims equal rights and duties.

623 CE / 2 AH
Muslims fight the polytheists of Makkah at the Battle of Badr.

624 CE / 2 AH
- The direction of prayer (*qiblah*) is changed from Jerusalem to the Ka'bah in Makkah.
- The first fast (*sawm*) is observed in the month of Ramadan.

627 CE / 5 AH
The Battle of the Trench (*Khandaq*). The Muslims are victorious when the Makkans and their Arab allies are forced to lift their siege of Madinah.

628 CE / 6 AH
- The religious duty of Pilgrimage to Makkah (*Hajj*) is instituted.
- The Truce of Hudaybiyah secures peaceful relations for 10 years between Madinah and the Quraysh of Makkah.
- Neighbouring rulers are invited to accept Islam.

628 CE / 7 AH
After a siege, the Muslims conquer the oasis of Khaybar.

629 CE / 8 AH
- Battle of Mu'tah between the Muslims and local tribes allied with clients of the Byzantine Empire. Khalid ibn al-Walid earns the title 'Sword of Allah' (*Sayf Allah*) for his extraordinary valour.
- The Quraysh violate the truce of Hudaybiyah by attacking the allies of the Prophet, the Banu Khuza'ah, at al-Watir.

630 CE / 8 AH
The Prophet's Conquest of Makkah in response to the Quraysh's violation of Hudaybiyah. He declares a general amnesty and his erstwhile enemies, impressed by his generosity, convert to Islam.

630 CE / 8 AH
The Battle of Hunayn. The Prophet launches a successful pre-emptive campaign against the tribes of Hawazin who were preparing to attack the Muslims. The tribes later convert to Islam.

630 CE / 9 AH
The Battle of Tabuk between the Muslims and the Ghassanids (an Arab Christian community). The Muslims take the poll-tax (*jizya*) without fighting and return victorious.

630–631 CE / 9 AH
Zakat is institutionalised and tax collectors are appointed and sent to the tribes outside Madinah.

631 CE / 9 AH
The Year of Delegations. Tribes from all over Arabia come to Madinah to accept Islam.

632 CE / 10 AH
- The Prophet performs the Farewell Pilgrimage (*Hajjat al-Wada'*) in Makkah.
- At 'Arafat, 100,000 Muslims gather to hear the Sermon of the Prophet where he announces the completion of his prophetic mission.

632 CE / 11 AH
The Prophet Muhammad dies and is buried in Madinah at the age of 63 on 8th June (12th Rabi' al-Awwal).

The Rightly Guided Caliphs

11-40 AH
632-661 CE

When the Prophet passed away, there could be no successor to his office of Prophethood, but the community elected some of his most loyal and closest Companions, such as Abu Bakr ibn Abi Quhafah, 'Umar ibn al-Khattab, 'Uthman ibn 'Affan, and 'Ali ibn Abi Talib as the Prophet's temporal successors or caliphs (*khulafa'*). These first four political leaders were collectively known as the Rightly-Guided Caliphs (*al-khulafa' al-rashidun*). They ruled the Islamic state and defended it, and propagated Islam beyond the Arabian peninsula. They also elaborated the administrative framework, founded garrison towns like Basrah, Kufah, Fustat and Jabiyah on the Golan Heights, appointed governors to various provinces, and paid salaries and pensions to soldiers, officers and citizens.

In the era of the Rightly-Guided Caliphs, Islamic power and authority was consolidated. Tribes that renounced fealty to the community and those who falsely claimed prophethood, like Musaylima ibn Habib, Tulayhah ibn Khuwaylid and Sajah, were opposed and defeated, which restored the unity of the Muslims. The first four caliphs, all elected through consultation (*shura*), contributed to the expansion of Islam, both within and outside Arabia.

Abu Bakr (*see page 20*), honouring one of the last commands of the Messenger of Allah, sent an expeditionary force to Syria led by the young non-Arab Muslim commander Usamah ibn Zayd. Abu Bakr's army defeated the Byzantines at the battle of Ajnadayn in southern Palestine. Abu Bakr nominated 'Umar to succeed him, and the community endorsed the decision wholeheartedly. Under 'Umar, his successor, the Muslim armies overwhelmed the Byzantine and Sasanian powers in Syria, Egypt, Iraq and Persia. A decadent 'old order' was replaced by a new social and political order of spiritual vigour and rejuvenation based on a strict form of monotheism.

The Death of Yazdagird III in 651

Illustration from the *Shahnameh* (*The Book of Kings*) by Firdawsi, pen and ink on vellum, Persian, fifteenth century

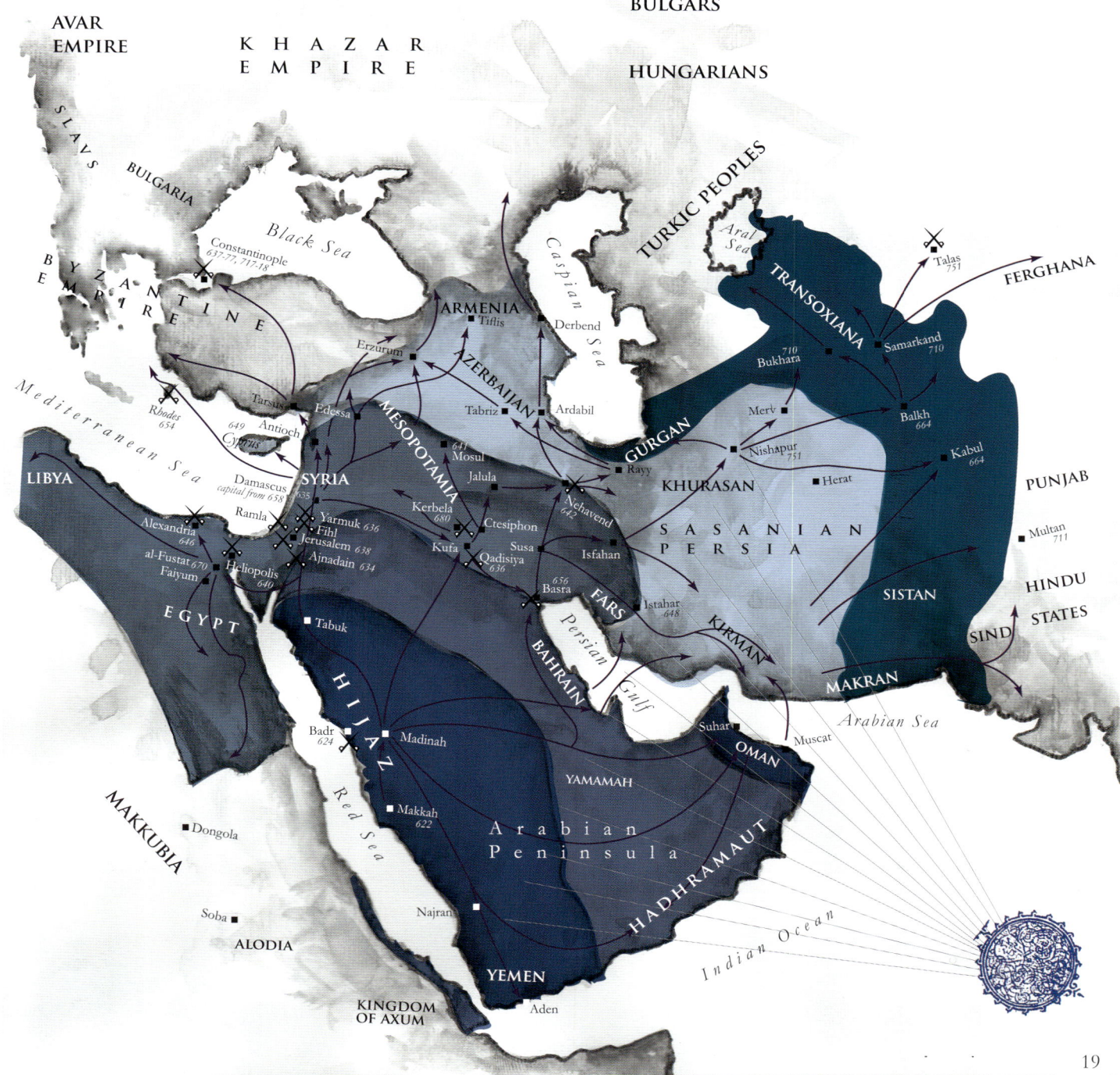

The Rightly-Guided Caliphs

Abu Bakr
632-634 CE/11-13 AH

'Umar
634-644 CE/13-23 AH

'Uthman
644-656 CE/24-35 AH

'Ali
656-661 CE/35-40 AH

- Under Muhammad
- Under Abu Bakr (632-634)
- Under 'Umar (634-644)
- Under 'Uthman (644-656) and 'Ali (656-661)
- Under the Umayyads (661-750)
- → Arab Advance
- ⚔ Battle Sites

Conquests of the Rightly-Guided Caliphs and the Umayyads

ABU BAKR
THE FIRST CALIPH IN ISLAM

Abu Bakr was the Prophet's closest Companion, his father-in-law, and the first caliph in Islam. He was given the title of the Veracious (al-Siddiq) by the Prophet himself. In the early days of the Prophet's mission in Makkah, Abu Bakr brought many to the faith and spent his wealth in freeing those Muslim slaves who were persecuted for their faith. When the Makkans doubted the truth of the Prophet's Journey to Jerusalem and the Ascension to the Heavens in one night, Abu Bakr was the first to affirm its veracity.

When Islam began to spread among the Makkans, the leaders of the Quraysh became increasingly worried, and so they came up with a plan to assassinate the Prophet. God then revealed the Quraysh's malicious intentions to the Prophet, and ordered him to leave Makkah at once. And it was Abu Bakr who accompanied him on that secret journey from Makkah to Madinah. That was the glorious *Hijrah* that marked the beginning of a decisive phase in Islamic history. On a calm night in the year 622, he and Abu Bakr left their beloved but now unsafe hometown of Makkah.

Arriving at the steep, rocky Mount Thawr, Muhammad's feet were worn out as they had walked on tip-toes to avoid leaving any trail for their enemies to follow. Abu Bakr climbed up the steep slope, carrying the Prophet. Seeking sanctuary in a cave, Abu Bakr feared that his beloved Prophet would be discovered by their enemies, but the Prophet reassured his great friend saying, 'Do not fear, for certainly God is with us', and they were miraculously protected from discovery.

Arriving safely at Madinah, for ten years Abu Bakr gave constant support to the Prophet, participating in all the great battles, and on many occasions giving tremendous financial support to the Muslim armies, until the Arab tribes had been unified. In 631, Abu Bakr became the first leader of the Hajj caravan, leading the pilgrims to Makkah.

At the time of the Prophet's passing away in 632, the community was bewildered by the loss of their beloved Messenger, and not even 'Umar, known for his great courage, could stand the situation, and at first denied the terrible news. Yet it was Abu Bakr who showed great faith and constancy in reminding the Muslims that, 'Whoever of you worshipped Muhammad, he is now dead, but whoever of you worship God, it is God Who will never die.' Abu Bakr's sagacity in these critical circumstances led to his popular selection as the first caliph of Islam.

Although he served as caliph for only two short years before his death in 634, Abu Bakr succeeded in subduing those Arab tribes that revolted, refusing to pay the obligatory charity (*zakat*), and he also initiated the invasions of Syria and Iraq. His famous first address as caliph reaffirmed the principle of justice in ideal political leadership: 'The weak among you shall be strong in my eyes until I secure his right if God wills; and the strong among you shall be weak in my eyes until I wrest the right from him.'

The Islamic Lunar Calendar

Each month in the Islamic lunar calendar first instituted in 637 is marked by the birth of the crescent moon

Sasanian War Helmet

THE RIGHTLY-GUIDED CALIPHS

632–634CE 11–13AH

Abu Bakr consolidates control of the Arab Peninsula

634–644CE 13–23AH

Under 'Umar the Muslims conquer Syria, Jerusalem, Egypt and Persia

'Umar institutes the Hijri lunar calendar

637CE 16AH

Further conquests in North Africa

644–656CE 23–35AH

The new leaders chose new sites to build the garrison towns of Basrah and Kufah in Iraq, Jabiyah in Syria, and Fustat in Egypt, whose newly-appointed governors, the flag-bearers of Islam, ran the branches of the central administration (*diwan*) at Madinah. They not only served as military chiefs and civilian administrators but also led the new and ever-expanding mosque congregations in prayer. It was a brand new empire set up by a tribal people who derived their inspiration from the Qur'an and the *Sunnah* of the noble Prophet, and who believed in brotherhood between themselves. They were a people imbued with a high moral spirit, but without any previous experience of running the affairs of an empire.

The epoch of the Rightly-Guided Caliphs (632-661) was an eventful chapter in world history that brought a new dawn of human development and spiritual progress in the ancient centres of civilization in Mesopotamia, Persia, Egypt, Syria and beyond. One of the most important achievements of this era was the use of four copyists, including a secretary of the Prophet, Zayd ibn Thabit, to write down the full text of the Holy Qur'an (*see page 24*). Another achievement was the establishment of the Islamic Calendar in 16th year of the migration (*hijrah*), dating back to the time of the Prophet's journey from Makkah to Madinah. With the Qur'an preserved and a vast empire

650–651CE 30AH

'Uthman orders that official copies of the Qur'an are made and distributed

656CE 35–36AH

Assassination of 'Uthman

656–661CE 35–40AH

Civil War between the Companions of the Prophet

Assassination of 'Ali
661CE 40AH

conquered and secured by a community educated by the Prophet, the future of the Islamic community was assured of rapid progress and continuing success.

The era of the Rightly-Guided Caliphs ended in political conflict between 656 and 661. Both 'Uthman and 'Ali were assassinated, and there were three major battles – of the Camel, at Siffin and Nahrawan – between groups of the Companions and new groups such as the Khawarij. The final outcome was the rise to power of the Umayyads. This conflict also gave rise to three major divisions within Islam – Sunnis, Shi'ahs as and the Khawarij – whose original dispute over the nature of rightful caliphal succession later came to be defined in theological terms as well.

THE COLLECTION OF THE QUR'AN

It goes without saying that the Qur'an is central to the lives of Muslims: they recite it in prayer, memorise it and try to live by its teachings. They believe it to be the very 'word of God' that was revealed to the Prophet. As such, for Muslims, the words of God can only be represented by the original Arabic: a translation into another language can be nothing other than an interpretation.

Memorization of the Qur'an by heart has always been central to its preservation, which God has 'made easy for remembrance', and the development of a strong memory was essential to the culture of the Arabs of the seventh century for it was their custom to memorize epic poetry thousands of verses long, as well as intricate family lineages. As the Qur'an was revealed in stages over 23 years, the Prophet trained a class of Qur'an memorizers among his Companions, whom he tasked with memorising the whole Book and teaching others.

For a period of 20 years after the Prophet's death, the Rightly-Guided Caliphs who succeeded him, made a series of written collections of the Qur'an to supplement and standardise its ongoing preservation by the Qur'an memorizers (*Huffaz*). During the caliphate of Abu Bakr (r. 632-634), 70 of the most prominent Qur'an memorizers were killed at the battle of Yamamah. Acting upon 'Umar's advice, Abu Bakr ordered the compilation of the whole Qur'an into one book, fearing its loss. The Prophet's former secretary Zayd ibn Thabit, himself a *Hafiz*, 'gathered the Qur'an from various parchments and pieces of bone and from the chests of men', although written sources were only

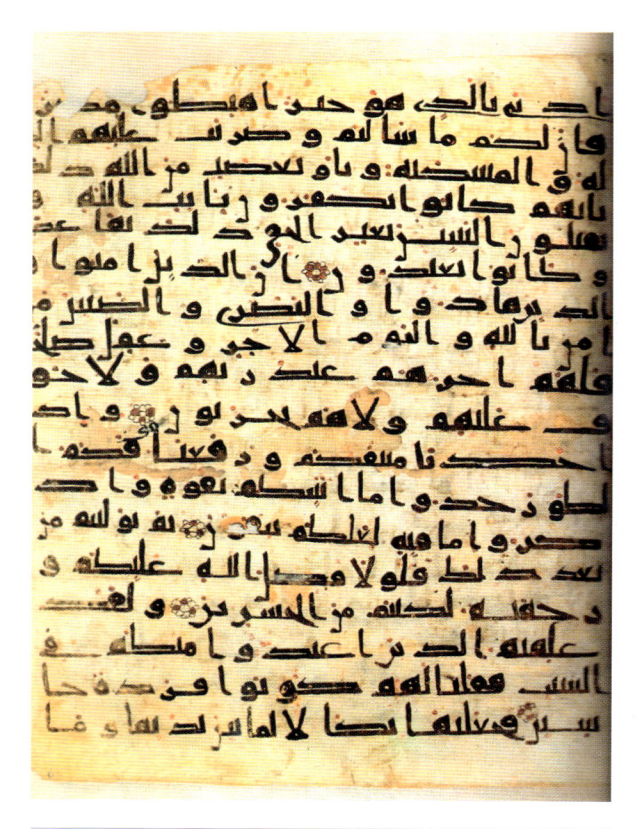

'Uthman's Recension of the Qur'an in Hijazi script

accepted if they were verified by two memorizers. The final copy was kept by Abu Bakr and later by Hafsah, the daughter of the second caliph, 'Umar.

By the caliphate of 'Uthman (r. 644-656), the Muslim armies had conquered many lands, and the Muslim soldiers reported that there were dialectical differences in Qur'an recitation among them, which had the potential to create disagreements and quarrels. Therefore 'Uthman ordered that a standard copy of the Qur'an in the dialect and recitation of the Quraysh be made from first compilation that Hafsah had kept. In 650-651, official copies were made and teachers were sent out with them to the mosques of Makkah, Madinah, Basrah, Kufah, Fustat and San'a'; the order was also given to destroy variant copies in other dialects.

The whole process from the first revelation to the final codification of the Qur'an took no more than 40 years. Muslims believe that God's promise to preserve His Book was manifested in the extreme care and accuracy with which the Qur'an was compiled and codified, eliminating any risk of errors or omissions creeping in, and allowing Muslims to have the fullest confidence in the veracity of their Holy Book.

TIMELINE
THE RIGHTLY-GUIDED CALIPHS

FIRST CENTURY AH
SEVENTH CENTURY CE

632–634 CE / 11–13 AH
Reign of Abu Bakr al-Siddiq, the first Caliph (*Khalifah*). He fights the War of Apostasy (*Harb al-Riddah*) and reconquers Arabia (*see page 20*).

633 CE / 12 AH
Khalid ibn al-Walid defeats the false Prophet Musaylimah in the battle of 'Aqraba' at Yamamah, in central Arabia.

633 CE / 12 AH
Abu Bakr dispatches three armies under Shurahbil, 'Amr ibn al-'As and Yazid ibn Abi Sufyan to conquer Syria.

634 CE / 13 AH
'Amr b. al-'As defeats the Byzantine army at Ajnadayn in southern Palestine.

634 CE / 13 AH
'Umar ibn al-Khattab becomes the second Caliph.

635 CE / 14 AH
Damascus in Syria falls to the Muslims.

636 CE / 15 AH
The Muslims led by Abu 'Ubaydah ibn al-Jarrah defeat the Byzantines at the battle of Yarmuk.

637 CE / 16 AH
The Muslims led by Sa'd ibn Abi Waqqas defeat the Sasanian army at the Battle of Qadisiyyah in southern Iraq.

637 CE / 16 AH
'Umar institutes the Hijri calendar.

638 CE / 17 AH
The Muslims led by 'Umar conquer Jerusalem, and pledge to protect the religious rights of its inhabitants.

641 CE / 20 AH
The Muslims under 'Amr ibn al-'As conquer Egypt.

641–729 CE / 20–111 AH
Life of the poet al-Farazdaq, who composed long poems in *Naqa'id Jarir wa'l-Farazdaq*, criticizing his rival Jarir.

642 CE / 21 AH
The Battle of Nihadwand. The defeat of the Persians leads to the Muslim conquest of the Sasanian Empire. Yazdajird III, the last Sasanian emperor, is killed in Khurasan.

644 CE / 23 AH
- 'Umar appoints a council (*shura*) of six senior Companions of the Prophet to elect the next Caliph.
- Assassination of 'Umar by a Persian prisoner of war, Abu Lu'lu'ah al-Majusi.

644 CE / 24 AH
'Uthman ibn 'Affan is elected as the third Caliph by the council.

FIRST CENTURY AH
SEVENTH CENTURY CE

644–656 CE / 23–35 AH
- Further conquests in North Africa under 'Abd Allah ibn Sa'd Abi Sarh.
- Successful raids in the East under 'Abd Allah ibn 'Amir ibn Qurayz bring enormous booty to Madinah.

645 CE / 24 AH
Death of al-Khansa, the most famous Arab poetess, known for her poetic lamentations for her two deceased brothers. She later converts to Islam.

646 CE / 25 AH
Death of the poet Ka'b ibn Zuhayr. His early work satirised Islam but, on his conversion, the Prophet gave him his mantle (*burda*) to Ka'b for a *qasidah* he wrote in praise of him.

645 CE / 24 AH
Muslim naval attack and conquest of Cyprus.

646 CE / 25 AH
'Uthman appoints a committee to write down accurate and officially-endorsed copies of the Qur'an (*see page 24*).

653–732 CE / 33–114 AH
Life of the poet Jarir, famous for his feud with rival poets al-Farazdaq and al-Akhtal and his satirical and eulogistic verse.

655 CE / 35 AH
The Arab navy defeats the Byzantines in the Eastern Mediterranean.

656 CE / 35–36 AH
- Assassination of 'Uthman in a conspiracy led by 'Abdullah ibn Saba'.
- 'Ali ibn Abu Talib becomes the fourth Caliph in Madinah.
- The Battle of the Camel. 'A'ishah, the Prophet's widow, Talha and Zubayr lead an uprising against 'Ali for not avenging 'Uthman's murder. An agreement is nearly reached when the party of Abdullah ibn Saba' begins fighting, leading to victory for 'Ali's forces.

657–658 CE / 37–38 AH
The Battle of Siffin between 'Ali and the Syrian governor Mu'awiyah ibn Abi Sufyan. They agree to arbitrate, but a group of 'Ali's supporters reject the notion of arbitration and cede from his camp. This marks the rise of the Khawarij.

658 CE / 38 AH
'Ali defeats the Khawarij at the battle of al-Nahrawan.

661 CE / 40 AH
- Assassination of 'Ali at Kufah by a Khariji fanatic and he is succeeded by his eldest son, al-Hasan.
- After six months, al-Hasan abdicates in favour of Mu'awiyah and retires from politics.

The Umayyads

41-132 AH
661-750 CE

The era of Rightly-guided Caliphs was followed by the period of Umayyad rule (661-750). The founder of this dynasty was Mu'awiyah ibn Abi Sufyan, a later Companion of the Prophet and a resourceful politician, who was initially appointed the governor of Syria by 'Umar and who continued in that office under 'Uthman and 'Ali. One of his main military achievements was the creation of a navy to challenge the Byzantine fleet in the Eastern Mediterranean. This Muslim navy conquered the islands of Cyprus and Crete, and besieged the Byzantine capital Constantinople between 674 and 679. As Mu'awiyah's governor of North Africa, 'Uqbah ibn Nafi' fought the Berber tribes, and founded the garrison town of Qayrawan in Ifriqiyah (modern-day Tunisia) in 670, which became the essential springboard for conquering the rest of North Africa. Qayrawan (now Kairouan) was also the first major Islamic city of the Maghrib or the Arab West.

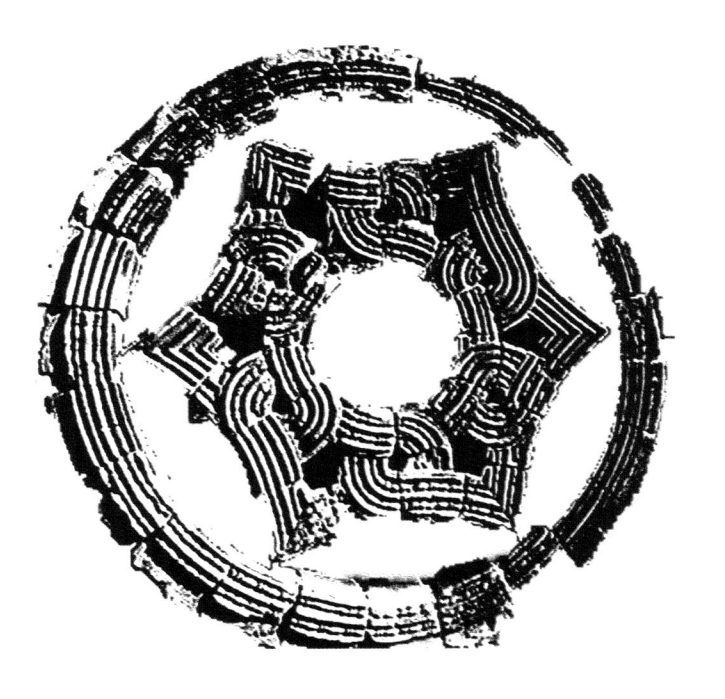

Under the Umayyad Caliphate, the very important political principle of electing a successor was replaced by hereditary succession. Mu'awiyah's appointment of his son Yazid as his successor marked this shift towards dynastic rule; early opposition to Umayyad control was manifested in the uprising of 'Ali's younger son al-Husayn against Yazid in 780. Thereafter caliphs were appointed on the basis of lineage or power politics, and the principle of consultation was lost.

During the Umayyad era, the Arab-dominated political leadership often pursued discriminatory policies that alienated non-Arab Muslims, especially the clients (*mawali*), or those Muslims who were adopted into one of the Arab tribes, but who were not always treated as social equals or regarded as compatible in marriage or treated equally with regard to appointments, promotions or salaries.

Apart from Mu'awiyah I, the Umayyad dynasty produced many able and talented rulers, including 'Abd al-Malik ibn Marwan (r. 685-705), al-Walid ibn 'Abd al-Malik (r. 705-715), Sulayman ibn 'Abd al-Malik (r. 715-170), 'Umar ibn 'Abd al-Aziz (r.717-720) (*see page 35*), and Hisham ibn 'Abd al-Malik (r. 724-43). One of the most important Umayyad achievements was further territorial expansion, especially during al-Walid's reign. The whole of northwest Africa was conquered during the governorship of Musa ibn Nusayr (708-715) whose client Tariq ibn Ziyad crossed the Straits of Gibraltar in 711 with 7000 Arab and Berber soldiers, and defeated the Visigothic King Roderic at Rio Barbate. Facing an army that was five times as large as his, Tariq ibn Ziyad roused his troops with the following words, 'Men! Before you stands the enemy and the sea is at your backs. By Allah there is no escape for you but valour and resolution.' Despite these heavy odds, the Muslims won a decisive victory over the Visigoths. Tariq ibn Ziyad then swiftly conquered Cordoba, Ecija and Toledo. His stunning success was followed by the arrival of Musa ibn Nusayr, the governor-general of North Africa, who advanced on Seville with a huge army in July 712. The rest of Spain was conquered between 713 and 716. Until 756, Muslim Spain or al-Andalus remained a province of the Umayyad Empire of Damascus.

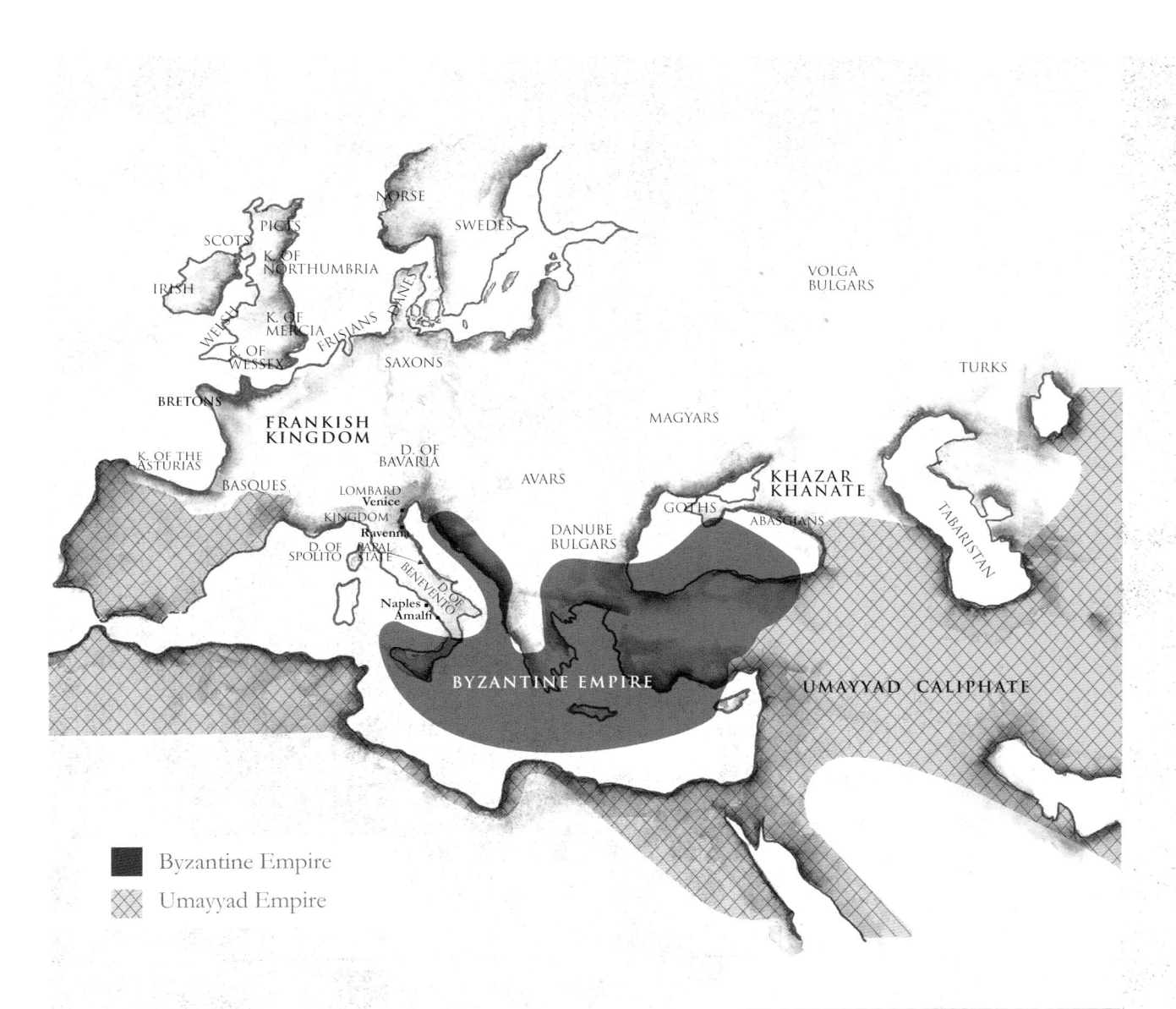

Umayyads of Syria

Muʻawiyah I ibn Abi Sufyan
661-680 CE/41-60 AH

Yazid I ibn Muʻawiyah
680-683 CE/60-64 AH

Muʻawiyah II ibn Yazid
683-684 CE/64 AH

Marwan ibn al-Hakam
684 CE/64-65 AH

ʻAbd al-Malik ibn Marwan
685-705 CE/65-86 AH

al-Walid I ibn ʻAbd al-Malik
705-715 CE/86-96 AH

Sulayman ibn ʻAbd al-Malik
715-717 CE/96-99 AH

ʻUmar II ibn ʻAbd al-ʻAziz
717-720 CE/99-101 AH

Yazid II ibn ʻAbd al-Malik
720-724 CE/101-105 AH

Hisham ibn ʻAbd al-Malik
724-743 CE/105-125 AH

al-Walid II ibn Yazid II
743-744 CE/125-126 AH

Yazid III ibn al-Walid I
744 CE/126 AH

Ibrahim ibn al-Walid I
744 CE/126-127 AH

Marwan II ibn Muhammad al-Himar
744-750 CE/127-132 AH

The Umayyad Empire in the year 737

661 CE 40 AH
Foundation of the Umayyad dynasty

683–692 CE 64–73 AH
'Abd Allah ibn Zubayr establishes a rival caliphate at Makkah

680 CE 61 AH
Husayn and his family are murdered at Karbala'

691–692 CE 72 AH
Completion of the Dome of the Rock in Jerusalem

Rock of Gibraltar
Named after Tariq ibn Ziyad who landed there in 711

An Umayyad governor named Samh occupied Narbonne and advanced towards Toulouse in France but his foray was repulsed. Despite such military reverses, other Muslim governors of Spain tried to conquer new areas of France. One of them was 'Abd al-Rahman al-Ghafiqi who advanced into central France and made his way north to Tours. Towards the end of October 732, Charles Martel, the leader of the Franks, advanced south to confront al-Ghafiqi and the two armies clashed between the towns of Tours and Poitiers. The Muslim army was routed and its leader was killed; the remaining army retreated to Narbonne. Muslims showed a continuous interest in the valley of Rhone and they were finally driven back by Charles Martel's army in 738. At the Battle of Tours – regarded as a decisive battle in world history – the tide of Muslim conquest in Western Europe was turned back.

The Umayyads of Damascus were not only famous for their impressive military victories in Central Asia, Caucasus, Asia Minor and North Africa and Southern Europe, but they built the first great works of Islamic architecture – the Dome of the Rock and the al-Aqsa' Mosque at Jerusalem and the Umayyad Mosque of Damascus (*see page 32*).

The Umayyads were also responsible for minting the earliest silver and gold Islamic coins and introduced Arabic as the language of administration in Iraq, Syria, Egypt and Persia.

Construction of the Great Mosque in Damascus

706–715CE 86–96AH

Tariq ibn Ziyad invades Spain

711CE 92AH

732CE 114AH

Defeat of the Arabs in France by Charles Martel

Ending of the Umayyad dynasty by the 'Abbasids

750CE 133AH

Silver dirham of Hisham, c.742

It carries the Arabic Islamic inscriptions introduced into Umayyad coinage by his father, 'Abd al-Malik

Dome of the Rock, interior

Al-Aqsa' Mosque in Jerusalem

Dome of the Rock, exterior

THE UMAYYADS

The Umayyad Mosque of Damascus

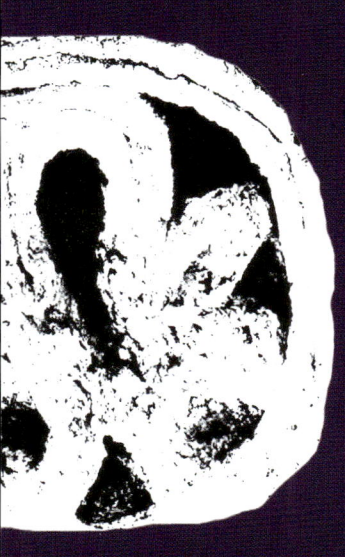

The first mosques had little or no decoration until the reign of Caliph 'Abd al-Malik (r. 685-705); the Prophet's Mosque in Madinah served as the centre of the community as well as a space of prayer, and was made of sun-dried mud bricks around a central courtyard, with porches on its northern and southern walls with palm trunk pillars and palm fronds for its thatched roofs. It had three features common to all later mosques: a place marked out for prayer, a roof to protect worshippers from the elements, and a means to show the *qiblah* or direction of prayer towards Makkah.

The Umayyad Mosque in Damascus, commissioned by al-Walid ibn 'Abd al-Malik in 705, retains much of its original appearance, despite the damage done by a great fire in 1893; the other great Umayyad mosques at Basrah and Kufah have not survived. Prior to this, Muslims and Christians had shared the site of the Syrian Roman Temple and Byzantine Church for prayers, but, as the number of worshippers increased, a larger mosque was needed to accommodate them, and al-Walid succeeded in his negotiations with the Christians to give up their part of the temple to allow the work of reconstruction to begin.

The original enclosing walls (157 x 100 metres) were retained and lined with arched arcades; a huge prayer hall was built against the southern wall that faced towards Makkah. Preserved today within the original walls is the Basilica of the Prophet Yahya, known to Christians as John the Baptist. Massive stone columns supported a wooden roof, with a screened space (*maqsurah*) that stood under the dome, incorporating the pulpit (*minbar*) and the niche (*mihrab*) for leading the prayers by the imam, which set the pattern for later mosque design.

Among the oldest surviving decorative features of the Mosque are six remaining delicately-carved marble plaques, and one magnificent naturalistic mosaic depicting a luscious forested landscape with pavilions and luxurious houses by the side of a river.

Façade of the transept of the Prayer Hall

Umayyad Mosque of Damascus, the scene depicted is a representation of Paradise

Other mosaics depicting paradisal scenes have not survived. Here the elaborate pictorial decoration of late Syrian Byzantine art is employed while respecting the Islamic prohibition of representing animate subjects. Supervised by al-Walid's brother, Sulayman, the work was begun in 706 and completed in 715, and, as well as local craftsmen, skilled labourers came from as far away as Egypt and Byzantium to work on the Mosque. In requesting 200 Greek labourers from the Byzantine Emperor, al-Walid wrote, 'I mean to build a mosque the like of which my predecessors never constructed, nor will my successors ever raise such a building.'

In the early days of Islam, mosques had religious, political, social, and educational roles too. In the Umayyad Mosque, the Caliph used to hold meetings and resolve disputes among the people. Its annexes housed the public treasury, the state arsenal, and collections of precious manuscripts. It was also busy with teachers and students, and was a place of advanced learning. Over time, schools and libraries were built around the Mosque, transforming the surrounding area into the equivalent of a modern university campus.

Umayyad Mosque of Damascus, courtyard

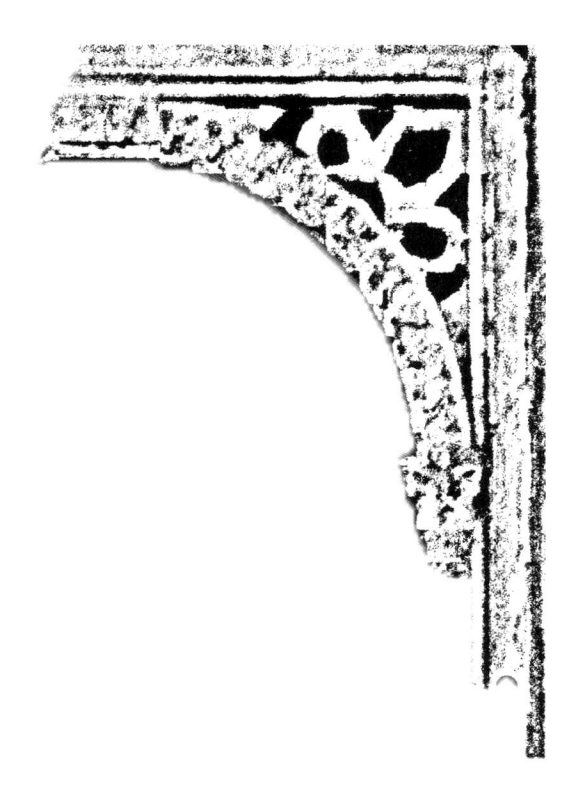

Among other achievements, one of their commanders, Muhammad ibn al-Qasim al-Thaqafi led an army to victory in Sind in the Indus Valley and Multan in the Punjab, both in present-day Pakistan. From 711 to 750, Sind remained under the control of successive Arab governors of the Umayyad dynasty. One of the Umayyad generals, Qutaybah ibn Muslim conquered Bukhara and Samarqand in Transoxiana and reached as far as Kashgarh. In 751, an Arab army fought against a Chinese force on the river Talas and captured some craftsmen who introduced paper-making to the Muslim world, firstly to Samarqand and later to other parts of the Muslim world.

Their unprecedented military conquests from Spain to the borders of China, consolidated by effective political rule, meant that the Umayyads laid the foundation for the spread of Islam and the further development of Islamic culture and civilisation. Much that came later was built upon the hardiness and mobility of the Muslim armies, the tactical brilliance of their generals, and the inspiration that they found in their faith. The Umayyads were, through the inspiration of Islam, able to rally non-Arabs to their cause: the armies that conquered North Africa, Spain and Central Asia were only partly Arab in composition.

Yet, even so, the Umayyads did not always live up to highest standards of equality and brotherhood in Islam. They could treat non-Arabs (*mawali*) as inferior and opposed groups with different political persuasions, such as the Zubayrids, Shi'is, Khawarij and the descendants of the family of 'Abbas. Their tough policies drove these opposition groups underground. The opposition parties formed a coalition and launched a secret movement to overthrow the Umayyads and bring to power an acceptable candidate from the Prophet's family.

'UMAR IBN 'ABD AL-'AZIZ
THE FIFTH RIGHTLY-GUIDED CALIPH

'Umar was born and raised in Madinah around 681. His father 'Abd al-'Aziz ibn Marwan ibn al-Hakam was the governor of Egypt, and his mother, Umm 'Asim, was the grand-daughter of 'Umar ibn al-Khattab, the second of the Rightly-Guided Caliphs. While growing up, 'Umar studied under the most distinguished scholars of his day, including some of the Prophet's Companions and became well-versed in jurisprudence and the traditions of the Prophet. 'Umar married his cousin Fatimah, the daughter of his uncle, the Caliph 'Abd al-Malik ibn Marwan, and then served as governor in Aleppo, Syria, and later as governor of Madinah during the reign of al-Walid, where he gained a reputation for ruling justly. When Sulayman ibn 'Abd al-Malik became caliph, he appointed 'Umar as his counsellor, and he nominated 'Umar to succeed him as caliph on his deathbed.

The stability of the Umayyad dynasty at the time, alongside his piety, experience of governance, and political influence, allowed 'Umar to make a large impact, despite the shortness of his two-and-a-half years as caliph. He appointed new governors with great care and monitored them closely, while allowing them the latitude to govern effectively. 'Umar II instituted strict controls to ensure that neither he nor his governors could exploit public funds for personal interest. As a result, state revenues increased and outstanding debts were paid off. Under 'Umar II, greater state support was given to the needy: the blind were given assistance, as well as the sick and the orphans. Allowances were granted to scholars, students, the muezzins and the families of prisoners; 'Umar II also established cash prizes of between 100 and 300 dirhams for outstanding scholarly works. War prisoners were ransomed, and the state sponsored marriages of the indigent. 'Umar II also ordered, against the Umayyad practice, that the *jizyah* (tax for protected peoples) should be lifted from non-Arab Muslims (*mawali*). However, 'Umar's most enduring project was the state-sponsored compilation and documentation of the Prophetic traditions. Copies of these documents were sent to all lands under his rule, which had a lasting impact.

In the light of his piety and services to the religion of Islam, 'Umar II came to be known as the fifth rightly-guided caliph. He died at a young age in 720, while still in his thirties, and proved during his short reign that the highest standards of Islam could be revived.

An Umayyad Storage Jar

Earthenware with a turquoise glaze, Western Iran or Iraq, 8th century CE

The ʿAbbasids

133-656 AH
750-1258 CE

The ʿAbbasid family came to power at the head of all the anti-Umayyad groups, bringing about the ʿAbbasid revolution, which aimed at the integration of all Muslim peoples – Arabs, Berbers, Persians, Afghans and Turks – within the vast territories under Muslim control, from Southern Europe to the borders of China. The ʿAbbasids implemented the *Shariʿah* (Islamic law) and sought to satisfy the aspirations of all Muslims. The early ʿAbbasid caliphate saw the establishment of a universal Islamic empire during the 200 years after 750, which enabled a golden age in Islamic culture and civilization.

After a century of successful, centralised rule between 749-861, under the first ten caliphs from Abu'l-'Abbas al-Saffah to Ja'far al-Mutawakkil, minor dynasties emerged – like the Saffarids of Sistan, the Samanids of Transoxiana, the Tahirids of Khurasan, the Aghlabids of Tunisia and others – that had much more regional autonomy.

The capital city of Baghdad was founded in 762 by al-Mansur, replacing Damascus, the capital under the Umayyads. The most famous and influential 'Abbasid caliph was Harun al-Rashid (r. 786-809), an able general, a pious benefactor and an enlightened patron of the arts, particularly of poetry, who was later romanticized in the *Thousand and One Nights* (*Alf Layla wa-Layla*). He fought valiantly against the Byzantine Empire and sent gifts to the emperor Charlemagne, most famously giving him an elephant, that caused wonderment in Germany, and a sophisticated water-clock, whose twelve brass balls struck the hour by falling on a cymbal (*see page 42*).

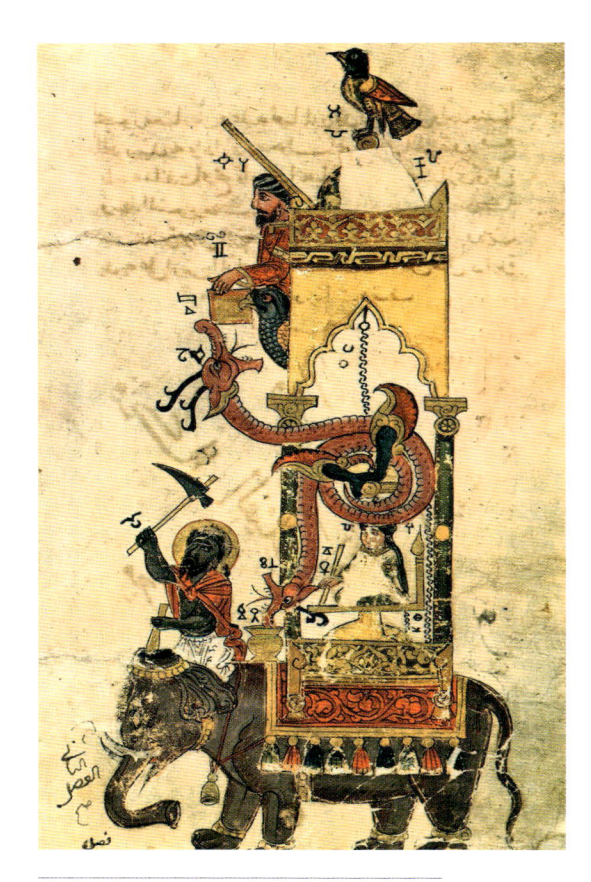

The Elephant Clock

The elephant clock of the twelfth-century engineer al-Jazari, which reflected the Indian, African, Chinese, Persian and Greek cultures that comprised the Islamic world.

The 'Abbasids (in Iraq and Baghdad)

Al-Saffah
749-754 CE/132-136 AH
Al-Mansur
754-775 CE/136-158 AH
Al-Mahdi
775-785 CE/158-169 AH
Al-Hadi
785-786 CE/169-170 AH
Harun al-Rashid
786-809 CE/170-193 AH
Al-Amin
809-813 CE/193-198 AH

Al-Ma'mun
813-833 CE/198-218 AH
Al-Mu'tasim
833-842 CE/218-227 AH
Al-Wathiq
842-847 CE/227-232 AH
Al-Mutawakkil
847-861 CE/232-247 AH
Al-Muntasir
861-862 CE/247-248 AH
Al-Muta'in
862-866 CE/248-252 AH

Al-Mu'tazz
866-869 CE/252-255 AH
Al-Muhtadi
869-870 CE/255-256 AH
Al-Mu'tamid
870-892 CE/256-279 AH
Al-Mu'tadid
892-902 CE/279-289 AH
Al-Muktafi
902-908 CE/289-295 AH

Al-Muqtadir
908-932 CE/295-320 AH
Al-Qahir
932-934 CE/320-322 AH
Al-Radi
934-940 CE/322-329 AH
Al-Muttaqi
940-944 CE/329-333 AH
Al-Mustakfi
944-946 CE/333-334 AH

Al-Muti'
946-974 CE/334-363 AH
Al-Ta'i'
974-991 CE/363-381 AH
Al-Qadir
991-1031 CE/381-422 AH
Al-Qa'im
1031-1075 CE/422-467 AH
Al-Muqtadi
1075-1094 CE/467-487 AH

Al-Mustazhir
1094-1118 CE/487-512 AH
Al-Mustarshid
1118-1135 CE/512-529 AH
Al-Rashid
1135-1136 CE/529-530 AH
Al-Muqtafi
1136-1160 CE/530-555 AH
Al-Mustanjid
1160-1170 CE/555-566 AH

Al-Mustadi'
1170-1180 CE/566-575 AH
Al-Nasir
1180-1225 CE/575-622 AH
Al-Zahir
1225-1226 CE/622-623 AH
Al-Mustansir
1226-1242 CE/623-640 AH
Al-Musta'sim
1242-1258 CE/640-656 AH

- Muslim expansion by 900
- Muslim expansion by 1300
- Muslim expansion by 1500
- Muslim expansion by 1700
- Muslim lands lost by 1300
- Muslim lands lost by 1500
- Muslim lands lost by 1700

The 'Abbasid Empire and its Successors, 750-1700

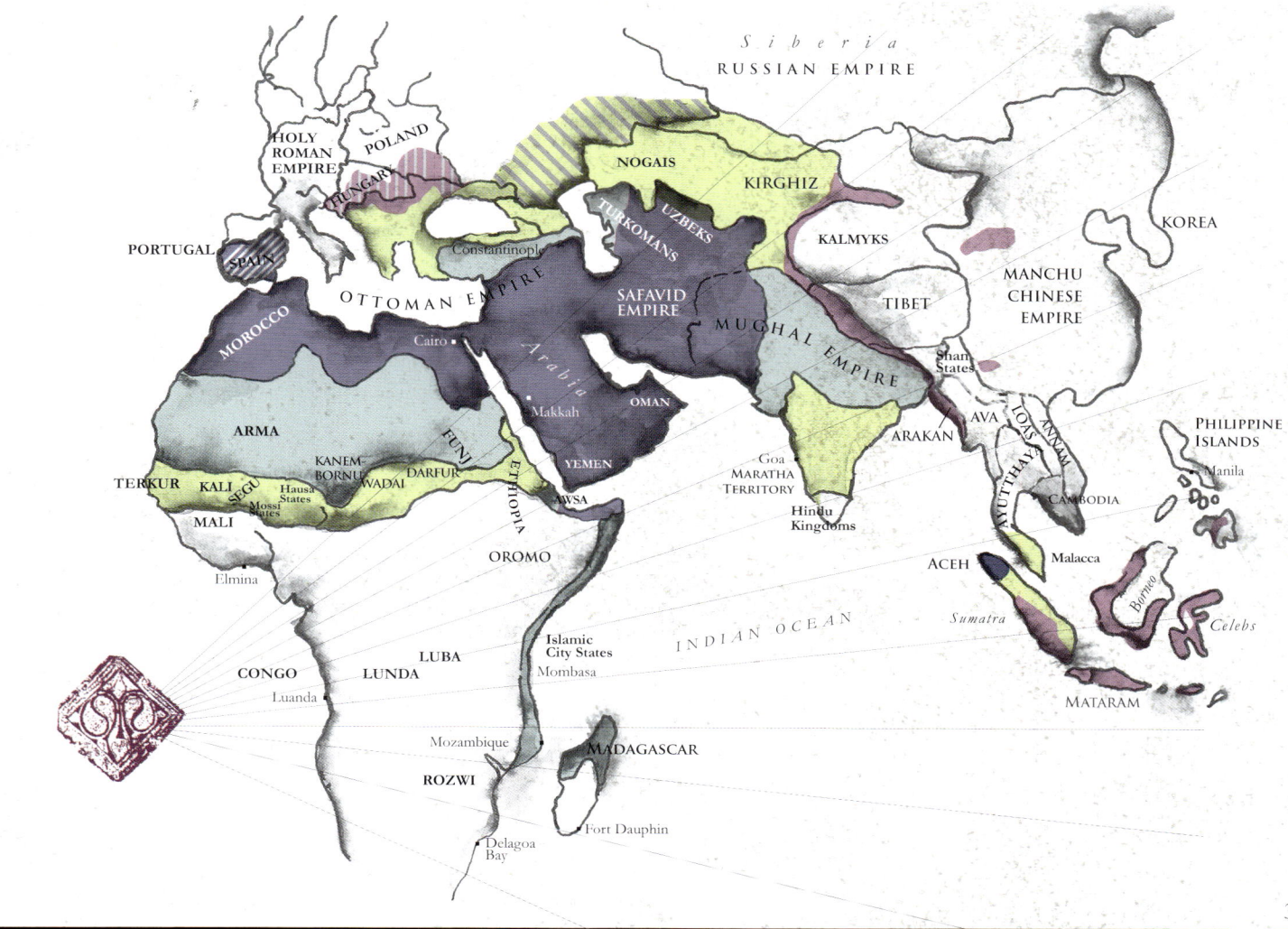

749CE **132AH**

'Abu'l-'Abbas al-Saffah becomes the first 'Abbasid caliph in Iraq

762CE **146AH**
Establishment of Baghdad as the new 'Abbasid capital

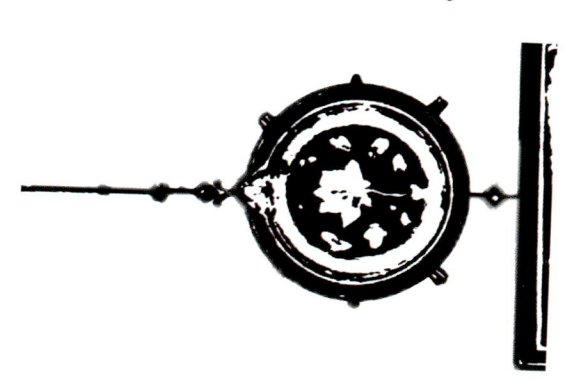

786–809CE **170–193AH**

Reign of Caliph Harun al-Rashid

801–873CE **185–259AH**
Life of the philosopher al-Kindi

Life of al-Bukhari, the great collector of Prophetic traditions

810–873CE **194–256AH**

'Abdallah al-Ma'mun (r. 813-833), the philosopher-king of the 'Abbasid dynasty and son of Harun al-Rashid, was a great champion of science, philosophy and rationalism. He was credited for his patronage of the House of Wisdom (*Bayt al-Hikmah*) in Baghdad, where the scientific and the philosophical heritage of the ancient world was translated into Arabic and interpreted within the framework of Islamic learning. Under the 'Abbasids, mathematics, medicine, astronomy, algebra, geometry, trigonometry and optics were developed and famous scientists and philosophers flourished like Jabir ibn Hayyan, Abu Ishaq al-Kindi, Ibn Sina, al-Biruni, al-Razi, Hunayn ibn Ishaq, Ibn al-Haytham, al-Farabi, Muhammad ibn Musa al-Khwarizmi, Banu Musa, Thabit ibn Qurra, Al-Battani, and many others. However, al-Ma'mun set himself against those ulema, or scholars of religion, who challenged what he saw as his caliphal right to pronounce on religious matters. He set up an inquiry (*mihna*) to ensure that all scholars and officials publicly support his view that the Qur'an was created. The jurist Ahmad ibn Hanbal's refusal to comply with al-Ma'mun's inquiry did much to reinforce the principle of the freedom of religious scholars from political interference.

The 'Abbasid caliphate lasted officially for more than five centuries (750-1258) during which the Islamic learning, like jurisprudence, theology, history, biography, linguistics and the science of Prophetic traditions (*Hadith*), were developed to a high standard. Interpretation of the Qur'an (*'ilm al-tafsir*) and the compilation of the Hadith collections, according to a critical method of authentication, such as the *Sahih* of Bukhari, *Sahih* of Muslim ibn Hajjaj, *Muwatta'* of Imam Malik, *Sunan Ibn Majah*, *Sunan al-Tirmidhi*, and the *Musnad Ahmad ibn Hanbal* were produced.

836CE 223AH — Establishment of the short-lived new 'Abbasid capital of Samarra in Iraq

839–923CE 225–311AH — Life of al-Tabari, the great historian and Qur'an commentator

865–925CE 251–313AH — Life of the physician and philsopher al-Razi (Razes)

870–951CE 256–339AH — Life of the philosopher al-Farabi

874CE 260AH — The first dedicated hospital is built in Cairo

Madrasah Nizam al-Mulk

One of the eleventh-century *madrasah*s established by Nizam al-Mulk, which did much to promote the Sunni religious curriculum

It was also during the 'Abbasid era that Islamic literature flourished. Great Muslim jurists, like Abu Hanifah Nu'man ibn Thabit, Malik ibn Anas, Awza'i and Muhammad al-Shafi'i and Ahmad ibn Hanbal enriched jurisprudence (*fiqh*), and great literary stylists such as al-Jahiz, al-Sistani and al-Tawhidi developed the genre of Arabic belles-lettres (*adab*) that intermingled various forms of knowledge from literature to science. The 'Abbasid period also produced many great works of history, such as Ahmad ibn Yahya al-Baladhuri's *Ansab al-Ashraf* and *Kitab Futuh al-Buldan*, al-Tabari's *History of the Prophets and Kings* (*Ta'rikh al-rusul wa'l-muluk*), Ibn al-Athir's *al-Kamil fi'l-Ta'rikh* and al-Khatib al-Baghdadi's *Ta'rikh Baghdad*, Ibn 'Asakir's *Ta'rikh Madinat Dimashq*, Bahshal's *Ta'rikh Wasit*, al-Ya'qubi's *Ta'rikh al-Ya'qubi* and Ibn al-Jawzi's *Kitab al-Muntazam*. Overall, despite political fragmentation between 950-1100 and later, driven by an industrial revolution in the production of paper, this was a 'golden age' of learning; the fragmentation of power led to the emergence of many courts that modelled themselves on the 'Abbasid patronage of learning.

When the 'Abbasid Empire shrunk with the rise of many minor dynasties and the power of the Caliphs was reduced, the Buwayhid Shi'i leaders (r. 945-1055) occupied Baghdad and appropriated executive power from the caliphs. Later, the Buwayhids were replaced by the Sunni Saljuq Turkish sultans (r.1055-1184). Nizam al-Mulk, the Saljuq vizier (*wazir*), founded the Nizamiyah Madrasah in Baghdad, where great Muslim theologians like Abu Hamid al-Ghazali, taught. Al-Ghazali produced great works of theology and philosophy such as the *Revival of the Islamic Sciences* (*Ihya' 'ulum al-din*) and the *Refutation of the Philosophers* (*Tahafut al-Falasifah*) that have remained influential in the definition of Sunni orthodoxy.

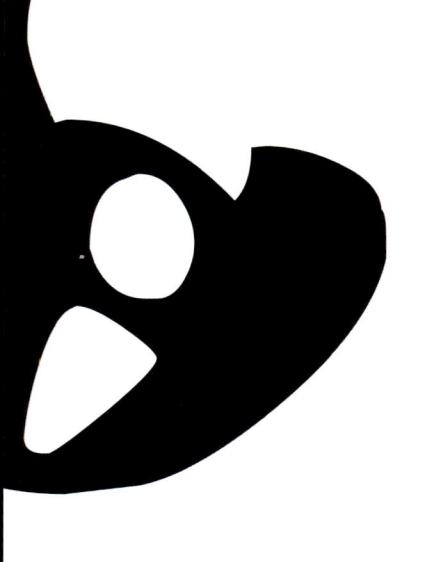

HARUN AL-RASHID
AND THE GOLDEN AGE OF BAGHDAD

The 23 years of Harun al-Rashid's reign are often seen as the 'golden age' of the 'Abbasid dynasty. Knowledge and the arts of civilization reached a peak, and Baghdad had grown to become the cosmopolitan centre of the grandest empire of the age.

Harun was born in Rayy, to the third 'Abbasid caliph al-Mahdi and his wife, Khayzuran of the Yemen. Growing up, Harun was accounted to be a brave and intelligent young man, who showed early promise. At the age of 16, he led successful campaigns against the Byzantines. The day that he would come into power was eagerly anticipated in Baghdad, and Harun came into his inheritance at the age of 22 upon the death of his brother al-Hadi.

In the early days of his reign, Harun appointed Yahya ibn Khalid al-Barmaki as his vizier, whom he sometimes referred to as his 'father'. Harun favoured the Barmaki family during his rule, and they became powerful during his reign. Yahya's son Ja'far also became a close companion of the caliph. The Barmakis' increasing power and privilege made them the subject of public criticism. Towards the end of his reign, al-Rashid became concerned by their influence and withdrew his patronage from them. This later became known as the 'tragedy of the Barmakis'.

Al-Rashid was a popular ruler who was widely seen as sincere. He reformed his administration, and worked to establish political stability and economic prosperity. With the installation of an effective postal system, and the construction of new roads serving the trading routes, everyday life was made easier in his time. Harun secured the borders of his land and established peace, chiefly by seeing off the serious military threat of the Byzantines.

Holding an interest in the intellectual life, al-Rashid patronized a scholarly movement whose principal activity was translating Persian, Indian and Greek scientific and scholarly learning from other languages into Arabic; Aristotle's *Physics*, for instance, was translated in Baghdad during his reign. Of course, this movement also produced Arab scholars of great originality in science and philosophy. The institution that was later to be described as the

House of Wisdom (*Bayt al-Hikmah*) saw the light under him as *Khizanat al-Hikmah* as a library of texts that he received as gifts or purchased himself. Under al-Ma'mun and his successors, it formed one of the most lasting civilisational legacies of the 'Abbasid dynasty. Hospitals practising Persian and Hellenic medicine were established in Baghdad during his reign.

Al-Rashid made nine pilgrimages to Makkah, more than any prior caliph. At his last pilgrimage, Harun pledged to secure the dynastic succession to forestall any future conflict. Witnessed by his two sons, al-Amin and al-Ma'mun, and many other witnesses, al-Amin, the younger son, was nominated to be Harun's successor. Al-Rashid's plan to divide responsibility between his two sons did not end well; instead, it led to rebellion and instability during al-Amin's reign (809-13) as each son came to lead rival factions.

Widely seen as one of the greatest Islamic rulers, Harun al-Rashid, died at the age of forty-three, of whom the enchanting tales of the *Thousand and One Nights* do little justice.

Water jug

Presented to Charlemagne by Harun al-Rashid, cloisonne enamel

---
House of Wisdom

The House of Wisdom (*Bayt al-Hikmah*) in 'Abbasid Baghdad

Harun al-Rashid

878CE **265AH**

The Arab occupation of Sicily

910CE **297AH**
The Fatimids gain control of Tunisia

The golden age of Islamic Spain, under the Umayyad caliphs of al-Andalusia

928–1031CE **315–422AH**

945–1055CE **334–447AH**

Baghdad captured by the Buyids; the 'Abbasid caliphs become figureheads

915–965CE **303–354AH**
Life of al-Mutanabi, regarded as the greatest Arab poet

THE 'ABBASIDS AND THE FRAGMENTATION OF POWER

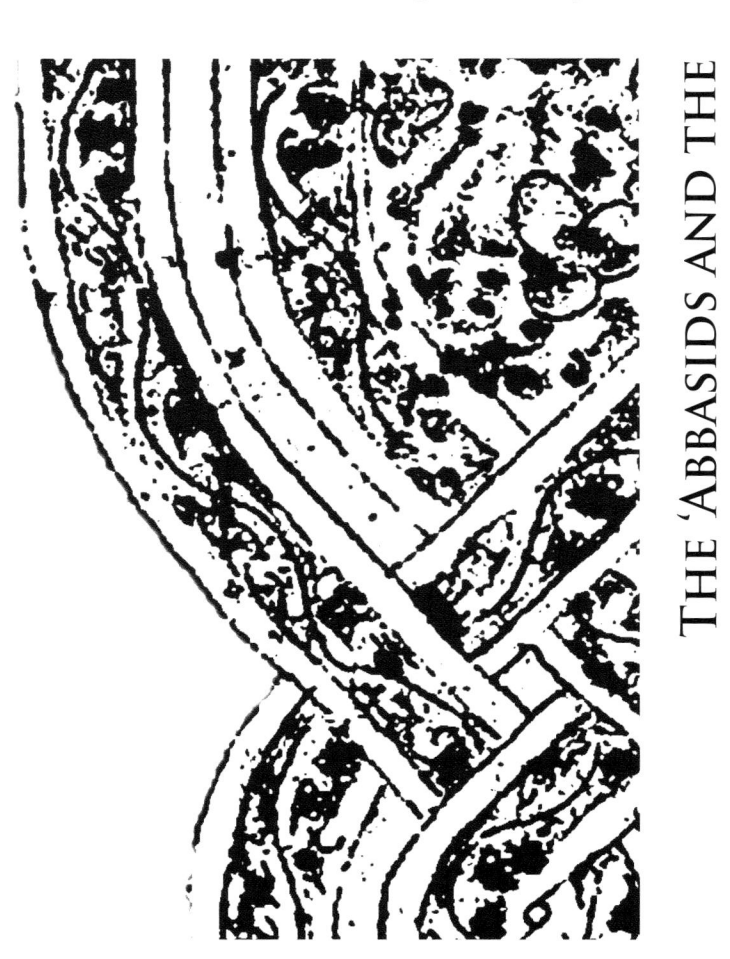

Despite the 'Abbasid overthrow the Umayyad dynasty of Damascus in 750, they could not control all the territories they had inherited from the former dynasty. As a result, within a century of 'Abbasid rule, a new political situation developed. It may be described as a fragmentation of power.

Consequently, although the early caliphs retained full control of central administration, their grip over the outlying provinces weakened progressively. By 945, the twenty-third 'Abbasid caliph, al-Mustakfi (r. 944-46) was forced to recognise the Buyid ruler, Mu'izz al-Dawla Ahmad, as the effective ruler of Iraq, and was then dethroned and imprisoned.

A JOURNEY THROUGH ISLAMIC HISTORY

878CE 265AH

The Fatimids gain control of Egypt, Palestine, Syria and the Hijaz

972CE 361AH

Foundation of the al-Azhar in Cairo

977–1186CE 366–582AH

Emergence of the Ghaznavids in Afghanistan, Iran and India

980–1037CE 370–428AH

Life of the philosopher and physician Ibn Sina

From 945 to 1258, the 'Abbasid caliphs exercised very little real power even in their own capital Baghdad; even if the office of caliph retained a symbolic prestige. After 945, the Shi'i Buyid (or Buwayhid) dynasty controlled Baghdad. They were deposed in 1055 by the Turkish Saljuqs who, from the reign of Tughril I onwards, ruled Iraq and Persia from Baghdad in the name of the caliph. During the reign of al-Nasir li-Din Allah (r. 1180-1225), the 'Abbasids were able to briefly recoup their lost power through a series of alliances, but this revival was insufficient to prevent the Mongol invasion of Baghdad and the fall of the 'Abbasid caliphate in 1258.

While they may be regarded as virtually autonomous, they were not a separate, independent dynasty like their rivals the Saffarids.

In the later centuries, many rival dynasties emerged that demonstrated the weakness of the 'Abbasid caliphate, but only the major ones – the Umayyads of Spain and later dynasties in Muslim Spain (r. 756-1492), the Idrisids in Morocco and their successors Almoravids and the Almohads, the Aghlabids (r. 800-909), the Samanids (r. 819-1005), the Saffarids (r. 861-1003), the Tulunids (r. 868-905), the Qarmatians (r. 899-1078), the Fatimids (r. 909-1171)

انقسام الحكم العباسي

The eastern provinces including Khurasan, Jurjan, Fars, Sistan and Transoxiana (Ma-wara' al-Nahr) remained under 'Abbasid control until the end of al-Mutawakkil's reign in 861. In subsequent years, there was a fragmentation of power in the eastern as well as the more central provinces. Some small dynasties remained faithful like the Tahirds of Khurasan (r. 821-91), who ruled from Nishapur as hereditary governors.

the Ikhshidids (r. 935-969), the Buwayhids (r. 945-1055), the Ghaznavids (r. 977-1186), the Saljuqs of Iraq and Persia (r. 1055-1194), and the Ayyubids (r. 1169-1260) – are mentioned here. Broadly speaking the eastern dynasties tended to recognise the 'Abbasids and co-operate with them while the western dynasties tended to be much more independent, with two of them – the Umayyads of al-Andalus and the Fatimids – setting up rival caliphates.

The Spiral Minaret of the Great Mosque of Samarra

Constructed between 848 and 852, the minaret is the only surviving part of what was the largest mosque in the world at Samarra in Iraq, which briefly replaced Baghdad as the capital of the 'Abbasid empire.

c.1000 c.390	Fragmentation of Muslim Spain into 22 petty dynasties		
Introduction of the lemon tree to Sicily and Spain	1031–1086CE 422–479AH		
	c.1011 c.401	Saljuq Turk invasions of the Middle East begin	1054CE 446AH
	Rise of the Ghurid Dynasty in Afghanistan and Persia	1037CE 428AH	Emergence of the Almoravids in North Africa

THE UMAYYADS OF SPAIN AND LATER DYNASTIES (756-1492)

When the Umayyads lost power in Damascus to the revolutionary uprising of the 'Abbasids, Spain was still regarded as a province of the Umayyad Empire. In 750, the 'Abbasid governor of Syria massacred some of the Umayyad princes. However, an Umayyad prince, 'Abd al-Rahman ibn Mu'awiyah al-Dakhil escaped and hid himself among the Berber tribes. Travelling in secret to Spain, 'Abd al-Rahman (r. 756-88) seized power to begin a new chapter in Umayyad history in Spain. His successors, some twenty-two princes, ruled over Spain from 756 to 1031.

The first two 'Abbasid Caliphs, Abu'l-'Abbas al-Saffah (r. 750-54) and Abu Ja'far al-Mansur (r. 754-775) failed to establish control over the Umayyad province of al-Andalus, allowing 'Abd al-Rahman I ibn Mu'awiyah al-Dakhil (756-788) to establish a new independent Umayyad dynasty, which ruled from Cordoba. The Umayyads of Spain came to be known as the Umayyad Emirate of al-Andalus. Under their rule, Muslim Spain remained outside the jurisdiction of the 'Abbasid caliphate, although in general North Africa (Ifriqiyah), with the exception of the Idrisids of Morocco, paid homage to the 'Abbasid caliphs whose names were still recited in the Friday sermons (*khutbah*).

In the tenth century, the sole claim of the 'Abbasids to the title of caliph was further challenged when the Umayyad prince of al-Andalus, 'Abd al-Rahman III al-Nasir li-Din Allah (r. 912-61) assumed the title himself in 929. In doing so, he also sought to oppose the claim laid by the Shi'i Fatimid dynasty (r. 909-1171) that controlled a substantial part North Africa and then Egypt from 969. The Umayyad caliphate of Spain ended in 1031, fragmenting through civil war into petty dynasties (*muluk al-tawa'if*), and afterwards loosing territory to the Christians in the north.

Included among the minor dynasties that arose in Spain were the Hammudids of Malaga (r. 1014-1056), the 'Abbadids of Seville (r. 1023- 95), the Zirids of Granada (r. 1013-1095), the Hudids of Saragossa (r. 1040- 1146), and the Nasrids or Banu al-Ahmar (r. 1232-1492) of Granada. Twice, Muslim dynasties in Morocco, the Almoravids (al-Murabitun) (r. 1062-1147) and the Almohads (al-Muwahhidun) (r. 1130-1269), sent armies to Spain to defend Muslim territories there against the threat of Castilian conquest. For certain periods, they established their own hegemony over the petty dynasties to prolong Muslim rule in the Iberian Peninsula until 1492.

1058–1111CE 450–505AH
Life of al-Ghazali, the influential theologian, jurist and mystic

1066CE 457AH
The Saljuqs found the first college, the Nizamiyyah, in Baghdad

1095CE 488AH
Pope Urban II calls for the First Crusade to capture the Holy Land

Spread of Islam in South-East Asia through trade

1100–1400CE 493–802AH

الامويه في الاندلس

Under Muslim rule, Spain flourished politically, intellectually and economically for eight centuries. Islamic culture was patronised by the Muslim rulers of al-Andalus. Islamic architecture and art prospered and Arabic and a form of Latin became the common languages of the Peninsula. The Arabs, Berbers, and Spanish converts to Islam created a new political and cultural environment that, with the full participation of Jews and Christians in commerce, administration and literary culture, produced Hispano-Arabic civilization (*see page 48*).

The pursuit of learning characterised Islamic Spain and many private and public libraries were founded. The great Arab rulers, such as 'Abd al-Rahman II (r. 822-52) and 'Abd al-Rahman III (r. 912-61), supported glittering courts where Arab poets, philosophers, scientists and physicians created the golden age of medieval Spanish culture.

It was in Spain that the great Arabic works of science like those of al-Khwarizmi, al-Razi, al-Kindi, Ibn Sina and many others were translated into Latin, from as early as the twelfth century. Among the scientists, physicians, philosophers and theologians who emerged in al-Andalus were Ibn Rushd (Averroes), Ibn Bajja (Avempace), Ibn Tufayl, al-Mu'taman ibn Hud, Al-Bitruji, Jabir ibn Aflad, Ibn 'Abd al-Barr and Ibn Hazm. However, despite its cultural and political greatness, the Muslims eventually lost power to the resurgent Christians who launched the Reconquista (Re-conquest) of Spain.

The arches of the Grand Mosque in Cordova, Spain

LIVING TOGETHER
TOLERANCE AND CREATIVITY IN MUSLIM SPAIN

Ousted by the 'Abbasids from Damascus in 750, one of the Umayyads re-established the glory of his family in Spain and between 756 and 1031, the Umayyads of al-Andalus created a remarkable society. They crafted one of the greatest examples of tolerance and cultural creativity in the pre-modern world through a spirit of convivencia or 'living together', which even outlasted the period of their rule, spreading in some ways across Muslim Spain to the Ta'ifa (or Petty Emirates) and then to Christian Europe. This was achieved through an inclusive interpretation of the doctrine of *dhimmah*, or the protection of the 'Peoples of the Book', the Jews and the Christians, under Muslim rule.

This spirit of 'living together' was not the outcome of formal political rights for minorities that are familiar today, but through the tacit acceptance that a state of complex and multiple identities within Andalusian-Islamic culture was accepted as a positive spur to creativity. It was a measure of confidence that non-Muslim cultures were accepted and engaged with creatively. The core medium of convivencia was the sophisticated Arabic literary culture, which was intellectually curious, open to creativity and everyday experience, and that did not set religious piety in opposition to this spirit of 'living'. Convivencia created a vibrant intellectual and cultural exchange between the Peoples of the Book. Arab poetry inspired a revival of Hebrew poetry in al-Andalus, which later shaped the troubadour traditions of southern France. It created massive intercultural cooperation that saw the translation into Latin of the scientific, medical, technological and philosophical advances produced within the Arabic tradition in the Eastern and Western wings of the Islamic world. This sophisticated learning, which was the most developed of its kind at that time, revolutionised European intellectual traditions and institutions of the day. For instance, this revolution shaped the thought of the master Catholic theologian Aquinas who built a synthesis

Maimonides

The great Jewish scholar and philosopher Maimonides who was born in Cordoba in 1135

of Greek Aristotlean philosophy and Christian theology in response to the work done by the Maliki jurist and philosopher Ibn Rushd and the great Jewish theologian, Moses Maimonides, both of whom came out of the culture of convivencia. Of course, convivencia should not be described uncritically in utopian terms, as it was not immune to outbursts of religious violence, the continuing distrust between Muslim, Christian and Jewish religious authorities, or the simple and pragmatic getting along among ordinary people, but it was nonetheless a remarkable achievement for its day and age.

While the cultural and intellectual legacy of convivencia survived the Umayyads and later on al-Andalus itself, as a lived reality, convivencia was weakened over time because of the continuous military tensions that accompanied the Reconquista and the rise of Crusader ideologies and that provoked a more intolerant intellectual climate under the Almoravid and the Almohad dynasties than had been the case under the Umayyads of Spain.

As the historian Stanley Lane-Poole remarked, 'Every nation, it appears, has its time of growth and its period of efflorescence, after which comes the age of decay. As Greece fell, as Rome fell, as every ancient kingdom the world has known has risen, triumphed and fallen, so fell the Moors of Spain.'

The literary and intellectual development in Spain under the Arabs and Berbers contributed to the Renaissance in Europe. The opulence and dazzling architecture of Muslim monuments like the Mosque of Cordoba and the Alhambra complex are reminders of the artistic and aesthetic heights that the Muslims achieved in the Iberian Peninsula. It is no wonder, therefore, that when the Muslims lost power in al-Andalus that they remembered it with nostalgia as the Paradise Lost (*al-Firdaws al-Mafqud*).

Iberian Peninsula

Kingdoms of the Iberian Peninsula, 1248-1492

Rise of the Almohad
Dynasty in Morocco

1121–1130CE **515–524AH**

1126–1198CE **520–595AH**

Life of Ibn Rushd or Averroes,
the philosopher and jurist

Launch of the Second
Crusade by Pope Eugene III

1147CE **541AH**

1169–1260CE **564–659AH**

Reign of the Ayyubids
in Egypt and Syria

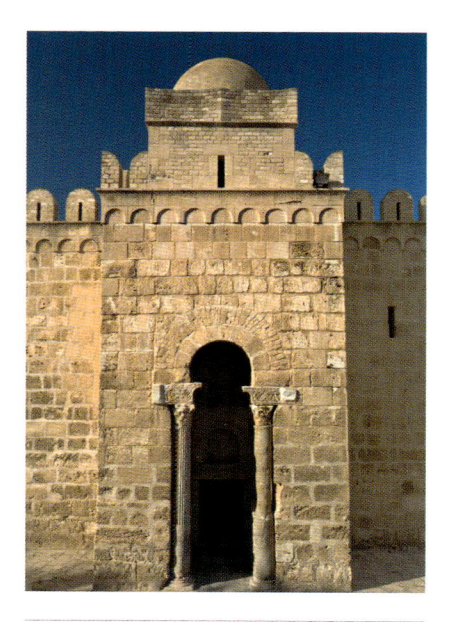

The Aghlabids (800–909)

الأغالبة

Another case of the fragmentation of political power was the rise of the autonomous Aghlabid governors of Tunisia and eastern Algeria (Ifriqiyah). Governor Ibrahim ibn al-Aghlab was granted the province of North Africa by the caliph Harun al-Rashid in return for an annual tribute of 40,000 dinars, which included rights of autonomy. The Aghlabids governed Tunisia and eastern Algeria and suppressed the sporadic Khawarij uprisings in their region. They successfully captured Sicily from the Byzantine Empire between 831 and 902. The Aghlabids had a strong fleet in central Mediterranean, enabling them to harry the coasts of southern Italy, Corsica and Sardinia. Malta was captured around 870 and it remained under Muslim rule for two centuries until the Normans conquered it in the later eleventh century. Malta and Sicily also played a significant role in the spread of Muslim culture to Christian Europe.

When the Aghlabids took over the administration of Ifriqiyah it was a Berber-speaking area, but, after a century of their rule, Tunisia had become an Arabic-speaking country. Subsequently, the rising power of the Fatimids brought an end to the Aghlabid rule in Ifriqiyah.

Aghlabid Entrance Gate

Aghlabid entrance gate to a ribat, Tunisia, ninth century, making use of Roman columns

1187CE 583AH

Salah al-Din defeats the Crusaders at Hattin and recaptures Jerusalem

1192CE 588AH

The unsuccessful Third Crusade ends with a peace treaty between Richard I of England and Salah al-Din

The engineer al-Jazari designs the ingenious elephant clock

1206CE 602AH

Reign of Genghis Khan, founder of the Mongol Empire

1206–1227CE 602–624AH

THE SAMANIDS (819–1005)

سامانیان

The Samanid dynasty emerged as the powerful governors in the east and great champions of Sunni Islam. It was founded by Ahmad I ibn Asad ibn Saman Khuda (r. 819-64), who was a governor of Farghana and Soghdia in Transoxiana. His successor, Nasr I ibn Ahmad (r. 864-92), was made governor of Transoxiana by the 'Abbasid caliph al-Mu'tamid (r. 870-92). They exercised power in the 'Abbasids' name in Khwarizm, Oxus and Sistan. On the death of the Samanid governor 'Abd al-Malik (r. 954-961) in 961, there were political revolts.

A commander of the Samanid army in Khurasan, Alptigin, tried to seize power, but, when his attempt failed, he fled with his troops to Ghazna in western Afghanistan. A number of nominal Samanid governors ruled there until 977, when Sebuktigin came to power. When the last Samanid ruler, Isma'il II al-Muntasir (r. 1000-1005) was killed in 1005, Sebuktigin became the independent governor of Ghazna.

Battle between Abul Qasim and the Samanid sultan Muntasir

Miniature from the *Jami' al-Tawarikh* of Rashid al-Din, c.1307, vellum

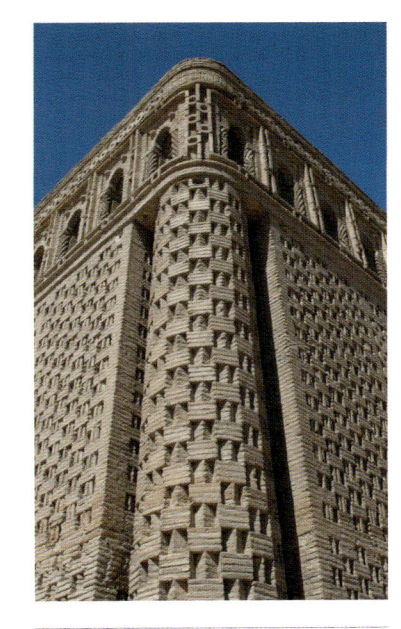

Mausoleum of Ahmad I

Mausoleum of Ahmad I, founder of the Samanid dynasty, Bukhara, Uzbekistan, tenth century

1243CE 641AH

The Mongols defeat the Saljuqs at Kose Dagh in Anatolia

1207–1273CE 604–672AH

Life of Rumi, the great Persian poet and mystic

The Saffarids (861-1003)

The Saffarid dynasty, which was founded by the Kharijite Ya'qub ibn al-Layth al-Saffar (r. 861-79) established his power base in Sistan and extended his control to Nishapur and Kabul. The Saffarid governors expressed contempt for the caliphs in Baghdad, taking advantage of the decline of the 'Abbasid power in the outlying provinces. 'Amr ibn al-Layth al-Saffar, who succeeded his brother Ya'qub, was recognised by the 'Abbasid caliph as his governor over several Persian provinces and, eventually, over Khorasan. Governor 'Amr ibn al-Layth al-Saffar (r. 875-882) looked to gain control of Transoxiana, which had been under Samanid control. However, the Samanid governor of Transoxiana, Isma'il ibn Ahmad (r. 892-907) defeated 'Amr in 900, and was rewarded the governorship of Khurasan, in succession to the Tahirids and the Saffarids.

Construction of the
Alhambra in Granada

1248–1354CE **646–752AH**

1258CE **656AH**

Fall of the 'Abbasid dynasty after
Mongul invasion of the Middle East

THE TULUNIDS (868–905)

طولونيون

An example of another independent governor was Ahmad ibn Tulun (r. 868-884), who founded the Tulunid dynasty (r. 868-905) in Egypt and Syria, and whose great mosque in Cairo was built in the Samarran style of his birthplace in Iraq. The Tulunids governed Egypt with a multi-ethnic army and a strong fleet. The 'Abbasid Caliph al-Mu'tadid granted Khumarawayh a thirty-year term of autonomous rule over Egypt in return for an annual tribute of 300,000 dinars.

Ibn Tulun Mosque, Cairo, 877

QARMATIANS (899–1078)

القرامطة

An extremist Shi'i group called the Qaramita, led by Abu Sa'id al-Jannabi founded an Isma'ili state in eastern Arabia in 899. Abu Sa'id captured al-Yamamah in 903 and raided as far south as Oman. In 930, his son, Abu Tahir Sulayman, captured Makkah during the pilgrimage (Hajj) season, massacring the pilgrims and took the sacred Black Stone (Hajar al-Aswad) from the Ka'bah to the province of al-Hasa'. After holding the Hajar al-Aswad for two decades, the Qarmatians returned it in 951 to be placed back at the corner of the Ka'bah after receiving a huge ransom from the 'Abbasid government.

The Black Stone

The Black Stone at the Ka'bah, taken by the Qarmatians in 929 and later recovered

The Fatimids (909–1171)

فاطم

These Shi'i leaders, who regarded the 'Abbasids as usurpers, felt persecuted in the 'Abbasid heartlands of 'Iraq and Persia, and sought to establish themselves as leaders of the Muslims in Ifriqiyah (eastern Algeria and Tunisia). By the use of Isma'ili propaganda, the Fatimids, led by 'Ubaydullah al-Mahdi (r. 909-934), won over the Kutama Berbers of eastern Algeria to their cause. With the help of the Berbers, the Fatimids overthrew the Aghlabid dynasty at Raqqadah, near the city of Qayrawan, and then the Rustamid rulers of Tahert in northern Africa.

The claim of the Fatimids to being descendants of the Prophet's daughter, Fatimah (may God be pleased with her), through the seventh Shi'i imam, Isma'il, is doubted by some historians. It is also claimed that the ancestors of 'Ubaydullah al-Mahdi originally came from an extremist Shi'i circle (*ghulat*) in Kufah. In 909, 'Ubaydullah was proclaimed caliph as a rival to the 'Abbasid caliphs of Baghdad. At first, the Fatimids ruled from Raqqadah, the former royal city of the Aghlabids, located in Tunisia.

In 916, 'Ubaydullah ordered the construction of a new city which became known as al-Mahdiyyah, the city of the Mahdi, which became an important port. His successor, Abu'l-Qasim Muhammad (r. 934-946), better known by his regal title al-Qa'im bi-Amrillah, built a powerful fleet to command the Mediterranean. His fleet further consolidated Fatimid rule in Sicily, and raided southern Italy as well as the port of Genoa in Lombardy in northern Italy. The next ruler, al-Mansur bi-Amrillah (r. 946-953), brought Sicily and Calabria under firm control and appointed al-Hasan ibn Ali al-Kalbi as governor of Sicily. The fourth Fatimid caliph, al-Mu'izz li-Din Allah (r. 953-975), regarded by some as wise and chivalrous, conquered Egypt, and founded his dynasty's new capital, the city Victorious or al-Qahirah (Cairo) and the al-Azhar Mosque in April 970.

Thereafter, a series of illustrious Fatimid caliphs, including al-Mu'izz, Abu Mansur al-'Aziz (r. 975-996) and Abu 'Ali al-Hakim (r. 996-1021) ruled over the Nile Valley, and their overlordship was recognised in north Africa, the Yemen, Hijaz, Palestine, Syria and Oman. Generally speaking, the Fatimids were tolerant by the standards of the day and appointed both Jews and Christians as their viziers, even if there were episodes of intolerance too. The Fatimids were also committed Isma'ilis, but they were content not to impose their views on the Sunni majority they ruled over in Egypt. However, Isma'ili doctrine was propagated among the families of palace and court officials, and the Fatimids were committed missionaries, sending preachers abroad as far as Sind in present-day Pakistan.

The al-Azhar Mosque was founded by the Fatimid caliph al-Mu'izz not only as Cairo's grand mosque but as a centre of learning, and it emerged as an extremely active intellectual centre and university in the Islamic world. Generally, science and education in Egypt prospered under the Fatimids. Ibn al-Haytham (Alhazen), the author of *Kitab al-Manazir*, advanced the science of optics, and influenced medieval scholars such as Roger Bacon and Johannes Kepler. 'Ammar ibn 'Ali advanced ophthalmology in his work on the treatment of the cataract. The Fatimid caliphs and their wives were famous for founding libraries, mosques and mausoleums. The al-Hakim Mosque, built between 990 and 1008, is well-known for its architectural innovations like the use of stalactite niches (*muqarnas*), inscriptions in Kufic calligraphy, and stonemasonry.

The Fatimids later collaborated with Nur al-Din Zangi, the ruler of Aleppo, against the Crusaders (*see page 64*) and their navy attacked Crusader castles and ports along the Syrian coast like Sidon, Tyre, Acre and 'Asqalan. In 1171, Salah al-Din al-Ayyubi ended the Fatimid caliphate and restored Sunni Islam and the recognition of 'Abbasid authority to Egypt.

The Azhar University, exterior

The Azhar University and Mosque in Cairo was founded by the Fatimids in 972

The Azhar University, interior

The Ikhshidids (935-969)

Abu Bakr Ikhshid, also known as Muhammad ibn Tughj, originated from a Turkish military family well-known for their service to the 'Abbasid Caliphs for two generations. He was appointed governor of Egypt in 935 and remained a faithful vassal until 946, securing the title of al-Ikhshid (prince or ruler) from 'Abbasid caliph al-Radi. However Ibn Tughj defended Damascus against attacks from the 'Abbasid commander-in-chief (amir al- umara') Muhammad ibn Ra'iq, and a rival dynasty, the Hamdanids of Syria. Ibn Tughj's successors were nominal rulers of Eygpt – the real power behind the throne between 946 and 968 being the Nubian general Kafur. The Ikhshidids were defeated by the invasion of the Isma'ili Fatimid general, Jawhar, in 969.

Fatimid Wooden Mihrab

Tenth century Egypt, with a Kufic inscription blessing the Prophet, his daughter Fatimah and the 12 Shi'ite Imams

The Buwayhids (945-1055)

There was a marked decline in 'Abbasid political power during the reign of the young caliph al-Muqtadir Billah (r. 908-932). Thereafter the Buwayhids, originally from the highlands of Daylam in Tabaristan and Gurgan rose to power, and emerged as an influential princely family, which had served in the army of Mardawij, the founder of the Zaydi–Ziyarid dynasty of Gilan. When Mardawij was assassinated in 943, the Buwayhids captured some of the western Persian provinces, and then in 945, the Buwayhid prince Ahmad ibn Buwayh led his army to Baghdad and set up a new regime which came to be known as the Buwayhid dynasty of governors (*amir*s). The 'Abbasid caliph conferred on the title of 'Amir al-Umara' (Commander of the Commanders) on the Buwayhid leader; the Buwayhid dynasty then imposed their *de facto* authority over Baghdad and Iraq for 110 years from 945 to 1055.

Although the Buwayhids were originally Zaydi (Fiver) Shi'is, they later converted to Twelver Shi'ism. Under Buwayhid tutelage, the 'Abbasid Caliphs lost their executive power. While the caliph's name was still recited in the Friday Sermon (*khutbah*), coinage continued to bear the caliphal stamp, and the drums (*nawbah*) were beaten in front of the 'Abbasid palace to mark the daily prayer, these were merely symbols of sovereign power. The Buwayhid princes, despite their control over the administration and the military, still paid homage to the 'Abbasids for fear of angering the people of Baghdad and Iraq, who were mostly Sunni.

The greatest Buwayhid prince was 'Adud al-Dawlah, who assumed the ancient Persian Sasanian royal title of Shahanshah (King of Kings). He built a hospital in Baghdad and patronised the literati and scientists. The Buwayhids were responsible for introducing major Shi'i festivals – the 10th of Muharram or 'Ashura and the Ghadir Khum in Dhu'l-Hijjah – as officially-sanctioned holidays. In 1055, the Buwayhids were overthrown by the Sunni Saljuqs.

The Ghaznavids (977-1186)

Under Sebuktigin (r. 977-997) the Ghaznavid dynasty was founded and under his son, Mahmud ibn Sebuktigin (r. 998-1030) a new chapter in Afghanistan's history was written. This ruler, known as Sultan Mahmud, launched summer raids on the Ganges valley in India and plundered its wealth. He built fabulous palaces in Ghazna and maintained a glittering court which patronized the scientist Abu al-Rayhan al-Biruni and the Persian poet al-Firdawsi, the author of *Shahnameh* (*see page 60*). Sultan Mahmud's seventeen raids against Indian kings weakened the economy and the political fabric of northern India, and paved the way for the Muslim invasion of India from Afghanistan and Central Asia in the following centuries.

Baba Hatim Tomb, Emam Sahib, Afghanistan

Sultan Mahmud was recognised by the 'Abbasid caliph of Baghdad, and he promoted Sunni Islam in Persia and Afghanistan. His armies marched against western Persia and overthrew the Shi'i Buwayhid military governors of Baghdad (r. 945-1055). Sultan Mahmud was also responsible for destroying the Samanids and dividing their territories. Officially, Sultan Mahmud was considered a vassal of the 'Abbasid Caliphs, although he acted independently.

Sultan Mahmud's successors clashed with the rising power of the Saljuq Turks in Persia. Sultan Mas'ud I ibn Mahmud was defeated by the Saljuq forces and driven out of Ghazna. Sultan Mahmud's dynasty had ruled over Afghanistan, Punjab, Baluchistan and North-west India. Ghaznavid power declined in the twelfth century and its capital, Ghazna, was sacked by the Ghurid 'Ala'uddin Husayn II in 1150.

Sultan Mahmud of Ghazna

Taken from an Afghan school textbook, 20th century

THE 'ABBASIDS

THE BOOK OF KINGS
FIRDAWSI'S *SHAHNAMEH*

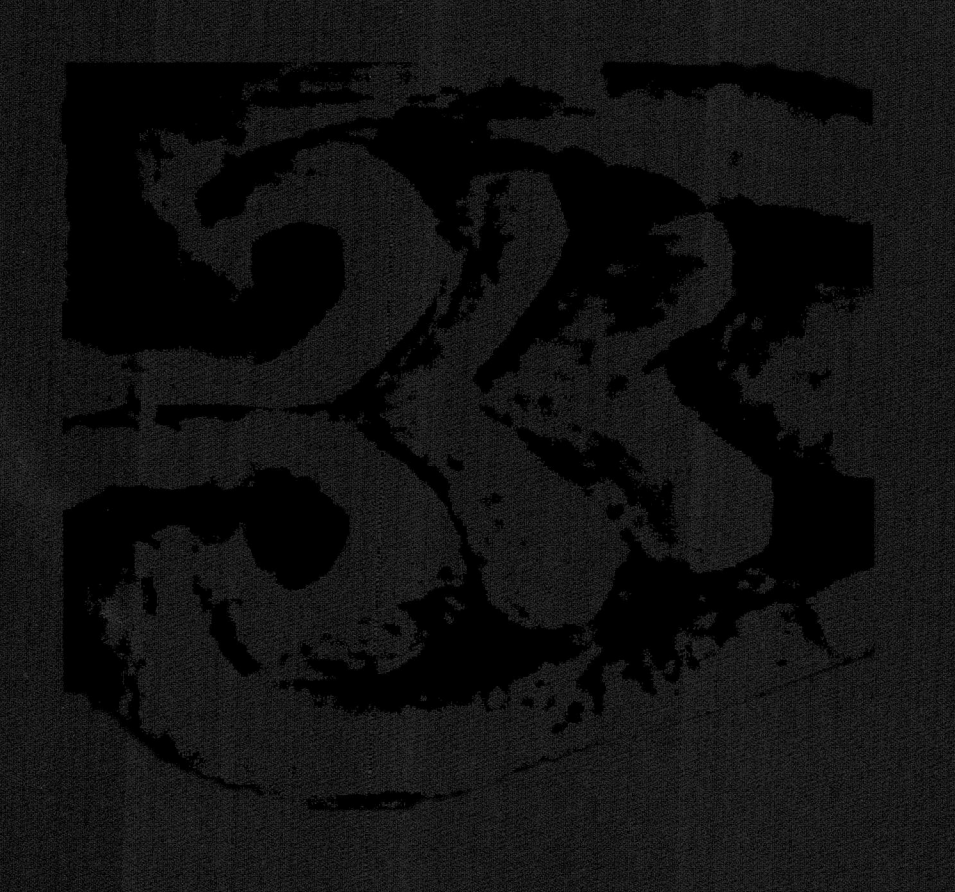

Abu'l-Qasim al-Mansur, known as Firdawsi (940-1020), was born in Tus. He lived in Transoxania, where the Samanids patronized Persian culture, art and literature, particularly in their capital, Bukhara. Amongst the most astonishing literary achievements of the day was Abu'l-Qasim's *Shahnameh* or *The Book of Kings*, which he dedicated to Sultan Mahmud of Ghaznah, who, as a former vassal of the Samanids, had by that time seized power from them.

It is largest epic poem ever written, containing over 60 stories, nearly a thousand chapters and 60,000 lines that exquisitely narrate the history and legends of Persia from the dawn of creation to the Islamic conquests of the year 641, which brought the fall of the Sassanid Empire; tradition has it that Abu'l-Qasim spent 35 years composing it. The *Shahnameh* celebrates Persian civilisation in elegant verse, with its tales of Persian history, rulers and heroes and its mixing together of mythological, legendary, and historical elements.

For the latter, Abu'l-Qasim drew upon ancient records of Persian history that had been recorded during the times of Anushirvan (Chosroe I) and then preserved orally by the old Persian landed families or *dihqan*s. The poem is also important to the Zoroastrians because it preserves the history of their religion.

Although Sultan Mahmud praised Abu'l-Qasim, dubbing him 'Firdawsi' because his poetry had turned the court into a gathering of paradise, the poet was disappointed with the paltry payment he received. Firdawsi then wrote a satire of the sultan and prudently fled into exile, where he composed his other great poem, *Yusuf and Zulaykha*.

The recurrent heroic figure of Rostam, known for his sly humour as well as his great strength and longevity, undertakes many heroic tasks as well as riding to the rescue of Iran in times of need, swinging a great mace. Rostam's tragedy is to fight his own brave and unrecognised son Sohrab in battle.

The *Shahnameh* is widely accounted to be among the classics of world literature alongside Homer's Greek epics, Dante's Divine Comedy and the plays of Shakespeare. The *Shahnameh* stands as Iran's national epic today for having shaped the development of the Persian language itself over the centuries, and has often been misused as a tool of political legitimacy by Iran's later dynasties, despite its far from uncritical celebration of kingship. The stories in the *Shahnameh* are still told at home to Iranian children up to this day.

Firdawsi, who died in poverty and embittered by royal neglect, nonetheless ended his great poem with the true prediction that all the land would talk of him, and that he would not truly die as 'those seeds I've sown will save my name and reputation from the grave'.

Rostam and Isfandiyar begin their combat

From Firdawsi's *Shahnameh*, Persian school, 17th century, vellum

A Sultan and his court

From Firdawsi's *Book of Kings*, illustration by Abu'l-Qasim Mansur Firdawsi (c.934-c.1330), gouache on paper

THE SALJUQS OF IRAQ AND PERSIA (1055-1194)

The Saljuqs were a princely family of Turks belonging to the Oghuzz Tribe of Central Asia, who rose to power during the mid-eleventh century during the power struggles between the Samanids (r. 819-1005), Ghaznavids (r. 977-1186) and the Qarakhanids (r. 992-1212).

Pushed into Khurasan by these struggles, the itinerant Saljuqs captured the province from the Ghaznavids and seized the city of Nishapur in 1038, where the Saljuq leader, Tughril Beg, proclaimed himself Sultan. In 1040, Tughril's Saljuq army decisively defeated the Ghaznavids at the battle of Dandanqan. The Saljuqs also successfully invaded Asia Minor, and Transcaucasia, including Abkhazia, in 1048.

Leaving his brother Changhri Beg in charge of Khurasan, Tughril Beg championed the cause of Sunni Islam and went on to liberate the 'Abbasid caliphate from the tutelage of the Shi'i Buwayhids by conquering Baghdad in 1055, where he was confirmed as sultan by the caliph.

The Saljuq Sultan Tughril Beg's name was recited alongside the Caliph's in the Friday sermon (*khutbah*) in Baghdad. When Tughril died childless in 1063, he was succeeded by his nephew, Alp Arslan, in 1071, who then went on to annihilate the Byzantine army at the battle of Manzikert. After the victory at Manzikert there was an influx of Turkish tribesmen into Asia Minor and in due course the Saljuq Sultanate of Rum was founded. When Alp Arslan died in 1073, he was succeeded by his son, Malik Shah who ruled for two decades (1073-92) and ushered in an era of glory and prosperity. His great wazir, the celebrated Nizam al-Mulk, guided the young Sultan, and founded the Nizamiyah Madrasah in Baghdad and Nishapur, promoting Sunni education all over Iraq, the Arabian Peninsula and Persia. Great scholars like al-Ghazali taught at the Nizamiyah in Baghdad.

At this time, the great Muslim scientist, poet and astronomer 'Umar Khayyam replaced the Persian Calendar with the Jalali calendar, which was more accurate than the Julian calendar in use in the Christian lands. The descendants of Malik Shah ruled in parts of the 'Abbasid Empire until 1194. There were many branches of the Saljuqid dynasty that ruled over Persia, Syria and Asia Minor.

The Ayyubids (1169-1260)

Najm al-Din Ayyub and Asad al-Din Shirkuh, who belonged to the Hadhbani tribe of the Kurds, were the progenitors of the Ayyubid dynasty. Zangi, the Turkish commander of Mosul and Aleppo, who had served the Saljuqs, recruited many Kurds into his army. Ayyub and his brother Shirkuh joined the military service of Zangi's celebrated son, Nur al-Din Zangi.

In 1169, Shirkuh was commissioned by Nur al-Din Zangi to lead an army against the Fatimids in Egypt. Shortly after his victory over the Fatimids, Shirkuh took control of Egypt on the death of the Fatimid Caliph al-'Adid. Shirkuh died shortly thereafter, and his nephew, Salah al-Din Ayyubi, was recognised as Shirkuh's successor.

It was a critical period in Islamic history. Syria was seriously threatened by the Crusaders, who occupied Jerusalem in 1199, massacred between seventy and ninety thousand Muslims, Jews and Samaritans, desecrated the al-Aqsa Mosque and mounted a cross on top of the Dome of the Rock. Zangi, and later his son, Nur al-Din, had led the counter-attack against the Crusaders, with some limited assistance from the militarily-weak 'Abbasid caliph al-Muqtafi (r. 1136-1160). Another Muslim hero of the Crusades was Salah al-Din Ayyubi who came to power serving under the Zangids (*see pagees 64 and 66*).

'Abbasid carved marble basin

Used for public ablutions (*wudu*) for congregational prayers, the twelve-sided rim is inscribed with the name and titles of the patron, the governor of Hama.

AN OVERVIEW OF THE CRUSADES

It may be necessary here to introduce a brief note on the Crusades, the importance of which has been generally exaggerated by Western historians. In fact, compared with the huge impact of the Mongol Ilkhanid invasion and rule of the Islamic East between 1256 and 1353, the Crusades were little more than a sideshow by comparison. The Crusades were essentially unprovoked wars of aggression by a number of disorderly Christian groups initially inspired by Pope Urban II of France to reconquer Jerusalem, which had been surrendered to Caliph 'Umar ibn al-Khattab in 638 and has since that time been under Muslim rule. The Crusades were partly triggered after the Saljuq sultan Alp Arslan defeated and captured the Byzantine emperor, Romanus Diogenes, in the battle of Malazgird in 1071 in Anatolia. Alarmed by this event, some Christians began a campaign to get support to defend Byzantium as the flag-bearers of Christendom. But it was only two decades later that Pope Urban in 1095 sent out a call to arms to European Christians, who responded by launching the First Crusade (1096-1102). The result was the unexpected Christian victory against the Syrian Muslims and the fall of Jerusalem, upon which the Latin Kingdom of Jerusalem was established, that lasted until the battle of Hattin in 1187, when Salah al-Din al-Ayyubi (Saladin) defeated the Crusaders and reconquered Jerusalem for the Muslims. His grant of amnesty to Jerusalem's Christians led to the promotion in Europe of Salah al-Din as a model of chivalry in battle. The remaining attacks on the Muslim powers of Syria and Egypt were eventful but failed to make a wide impact on the Muslim Middle East, for instance in cementing a successful alliance with the Mongols, or these forays ended in failure. By 1291, all European Christian territorial gains were eventually recaptured by the Ayyubid and Mamluk sultans, taking advantage too of Mongol weakness in Syria.

The Krak des Chevaliers

The citadel of the Knights of St. John in Syria

It is worth mentioning that the 'Abbasid caliphs had little role to play in defending the Muslim world against the Crusaders. Before the Crusades began, the 'Abbasids had lost political control over Syria and Egypt, the main territories of interest to the Crusaders, where the Fatimid caliphs (r. 909-1171), the Ayyubid sultans (r. 1169-1260) and the Mamluks (r. 1250-1517) ruled in succession. However, the 'Abbasid caliphs played an inspirational role in encouraging Muslim to participate in the struggle against the Crusaders.

Muslim historians only came to write about the Crusades separately much later on and considered them to be more significant when making comparisons with European colonialism in the nineteenth and twentieth centuries. At this point the Crusades became 'deeply etched in the Islamic consciousness' and became symbolic of the tension and distrust between Islam and the West.

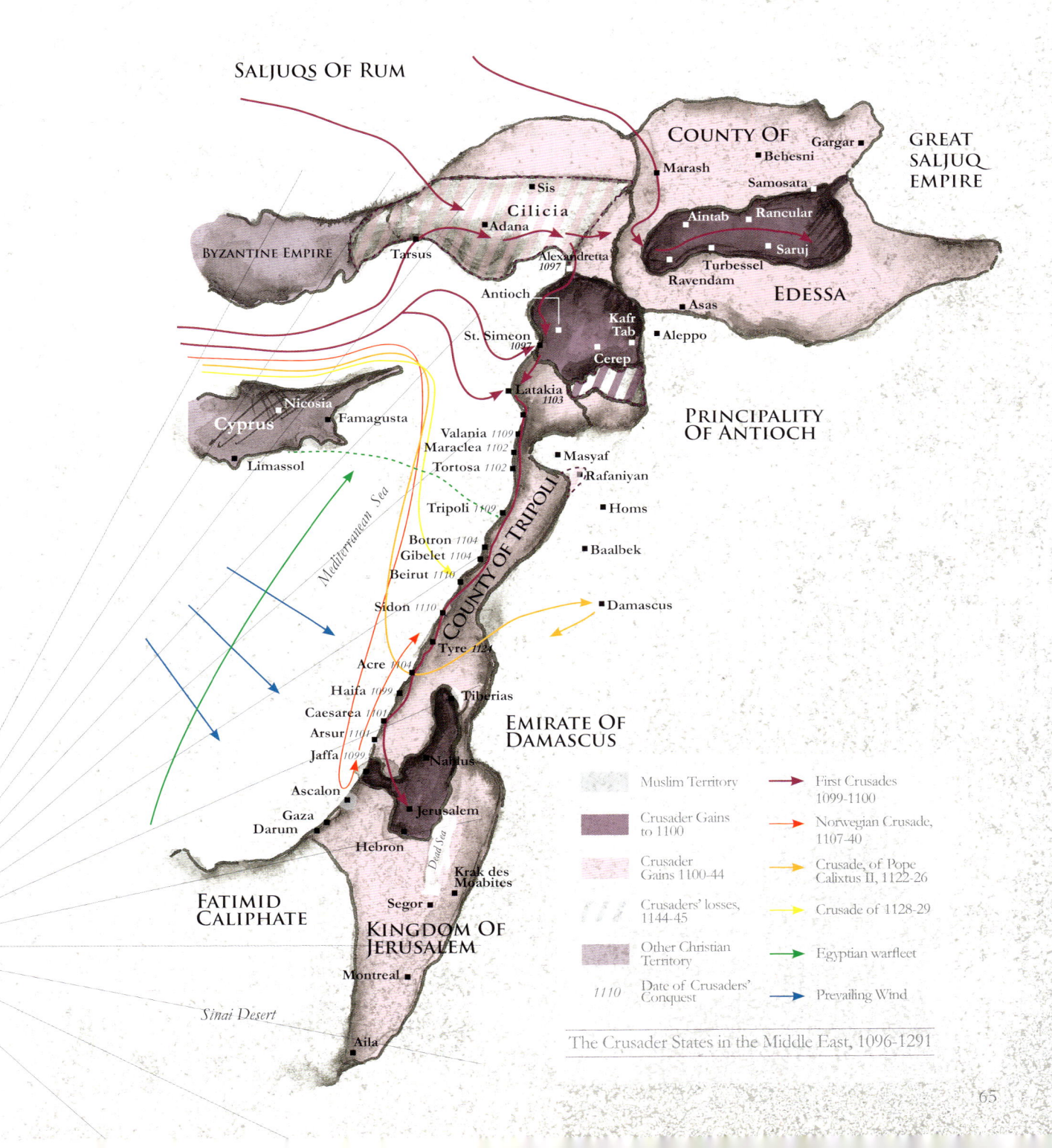

The Crusader States in the Middle East, 1096-1291

THE 'ABBASIDS

SALAH AL-DIN AL-AYYUBI DEFENDER OF ISLAM

Salah al-Din al-Ayyubi (1138-1193) was a great sultan who restored the dignity of the Sunni Muslim world by ending Isma'ili Fatimid rule in Egypt and turning back the threat of the European Crusaders, who had ruled what they called the Latin Kingdom of Jerusalem for 70 years. He is widely remembered in world history as a chivalrous king who dealt with his enemies with magnanimity and humanity. He was born in Tikrit in Iraq, the son of a high-ranking Kurdish soldier in the army of Nur al-Din, the Zangid ruler of Syria. He grew up to be a pious man whose mercy and kindness was apparent in all his military encounters with the Crusaders. At the age of 25, he was appointed governor of Alexandria, then, at 31, he was appointed minister of Egypt under the Fatimid ruler al-'Adid. Upon al-'Adid's death, Salah al-Din founded his own Ayyubid dynasty and thereafter ruled the Egyptians in the name of the 'Abbasid Caliphate of Baghdad. When the great Zangid leader Nur al-Din died, his dynasty disintegrated into factions, which allowed the opportunistic Crusaders to gain more influence. In an attempt to unite Muslims against the Crusader threat, Salah al-Din reunified the Zangid territories under his rule.

Salah al-Din is best known today for his victories against the armies of the Third Crusade. The Battle of Hattin is among the most famous of these, where 12,000 Muslim troops defeated 63,000 Crusaders, which opened the way for the recapture of 12 cities that had been under Crusader control. Among them was Jerusalem, which was liberated after 90 years without harm to its civilians and an amnesty for the defeated Crusaders. However, the Crusaders were not always so chivalrous themselves:

Salad al-Din's castle at 'Ajlun in Jordan

Salah al-Din's dirham

A silver dirham of Salah al-Din al-Ayyubi, dated 1182-3

the two-year Crusader siege of Akkah had ended in a truce, but it was broken and King Richard of England slaughtered its garrison of 3000 men.

Yet Salah al-Din was forgiving of Richard's crime: in a later skirmish, on hearing that Richard had lost his horse, he sent him a replacement with a message, 'it is not right that so courageous a warrior should have to fight on foot.' The Crusaders abandoned the attempt to reconquer Jerusalem, for Richard judged that so long as Salah al-Din remained its protector, they would never succeed. Salah al-Din and Richard then negotiated a truce of three years and three months on the grounds that the Muslims would keep Jerusalem and other cities, while the coastal cities remained under Crusader control. Richard then returned to England as a result of political instability in his kingdom.

Salah al-Din was not just a great general but also set about promoting higher education in Cairo, Jerusalem and Damascus and setting up courts of law. He did not view himself as being above the law, but bound by it himself. A merchant once filed a suit against Salah al-Din for seizing the property of a slave that he claimed belonged to him. The sultan appeared at the court and proved his rightful ownership and that the merchant's documents were forgeries; yet, even though he won the case, Salah al-Din gave the merchant a robe and money to cover his court expenses and affirmed that he held no personal enmity against him.

THE CALIPHATE AFTER THE 'ABBASIDS
(1258-1924)

After five centuries, the 'Abbasid caliphate was destroyed in 1258 by the Mongol leader, Hulagu Khan, a grandson of the Mongol military powerhouse, Chenghiz Khan of Mongolia. His armies, which swept through Central Asia, Iran, Iraq and Syria in five years, were described by the historian, al-Juwayni, as 'a mountain of iron'. The last 'Abbasid caliph, al-Musta'sim Billah (r. 1242-58), was wrapped in a carpet and trampled to death. The city of Baghdad was sacked, and one million of its population were mercilessly massacred. The contemporary historian, Ibn Wassaf, wrote that the Mongols swept through Baghdad 'like ravaging wolves attacking sheep'. Palaces, mosques and libraries were destroyed in an orgy of bloodshed, ending a glorious chapter in Islamic history. The Mongols were stopped at 'Ayn Jalut in Palestine in 1260 by the bravery of Egyptian Mamluks, whose victory prevented a strong alliance developing between the Crusaders and the Mongols.

The Mongols of the line of Hulagu Khan, known as the Ilkhanids, ruled over Persia, Iraq and part of Anatolia (r. 1256-1353). The cities of Tabriz and Maraghah served as their new capitals. After a generation, some Mongol rulers, such as Uljaytu, Ghazan Khan and Abu Sa'id converted to Islam, lost their appetite for savage warmongering and became civilized.

The Mamluks had replaced the Ayyubids as the rulers of Egypt and Syria. Sultan Baybars I installed a scion of the 'Abbasid caliphs of Baghdad, namely Abu'l-Qasim al-Muntasir (r. 1261-62) in Cairo. He was crowned with much fanfare as the new 'Abbasid caliph. Although the memory of the 'Abbasids of Baghdad was honoured, the 'Abbasid Caliphs of Cairo held little more than titular rather than official status, achieved limited recognition outside of Egypt, and were pensioned by the Mamluk sultans. Seventeen 'Abbasid shadow-caliphs held this title over a period of three centuries until 1517 when the Ottoman Turkish sultan Selim I defeated Qansaw al-Ghawri, the last Mamluk Sultan at Marj Dabiq in Syria in 1516. The following year Cairo and the Mamluk dynasty fell to the Turks. The last 'Abbasid shadow-caliph, Mutawwakil III, was taken to Constantinople, where he reportedly surrendered his title to Selim I, although whether this transfer of title should be taken at face value is doubted by historians.

The Ottomans, from the time of Murad II (r. 1446-1451) onwards, had sometimes used the title of caliph to strengthen their legitimacy, but they never made a formal and lasting claim to exercise political authority over all Muslims, regarding themselves first of all as sultans or kings. However, these claims were made more strongly in the late eighteenth century, when, in losing land to the Russians and other European nations, the title of caliph was emphasised to highlight the sultan's spiritual duty towards Muslims now under foreign non-Muslim rule. It was Abdulhamid II (r. 1876-1909) who made the strongest claim to the office of caliph again in the hope of shoring up support for an Ottoman empire that was rapidly loosing ground to the European powers and to growing nationalist sentiment within its borders. The caliphate was formally abolished by the nationalist Turkish leader Kemal Ataturk on 3rd March 1924. Its abolition was seen a great tragedy for the Muslim community (*ummah*) as a whole. For thirteen centuries, since the election of the first caliph, Abu Bakr al-Siddiq, in the year 632, the caliphate, despite its decline in political significance after the tenth century, remained the potent symbol of Muslim unity. The historical unified caliphate under the Rightly-guided caliphs, the Umayyads and the early 'Abbasids kept a great symbolic legitimacy right down to the beginning of the twentieth century and after, providing a political ideal and a challenge to the misconduct of Muslim kings and rulers throughout the ages.

The caliphate had come to symbolise the ideal model of political authority in Islam. Apart from the Sunnis, the Shi'i Muslims had established the Fatimid caliphate during the tenth century, a sign that the institution of the caliphate itself enjoyed near universal prestige among Muslims of all backgrounds and denominations throughout the fifteen centuries of Islamic history. It is for this reason that the abolition of the caliphate, even if it had become more a symbol of unity by the twentieth century, was still seen as a great loss by the vast majority of Muslims. It had widespread legal and spiritual consequences for the Muslim community (*ummah*): there is no caliph in whose name the Friday sermon (*khutbah*) can be delivered in mosques throughout the Muslim world. The loss of the caliph as a Muslim sovereign authority was in and of itself a sign of the sharp decline in Islamic power and authority by the twentieth century. The abolition of the caliphate by a nationalist government in Turkey showed that it was no longer regarded as a relevant institution, a dramatic change from the Ottomans in the late nineteenth century who had attempted to revive the office of the caliphate to order to strengthen Muslim unity.

The Mamluks

649-923 AH
1250-1517 CE

The Mamluk (literally 'Slave') dynasty of Egypt arose during the military crisis provoked by the Seventh Crusade under Louis IX of France and the Mongol invasion of Syria, replacing their former masters, the Ayyubids. At its height, Mamluk control stretched from Egypt to Cyrenaica in Libya to the west, Nubia to the south and the Taurus Mountains in the north.

The Mamluks originated from a Turkish military household of the Ayyubid ruler al-Malik al-Salih Najm in Egypt and Damascus, and they ruled for two-and-a-half centuries under two branches, namely the Bahriyyah (r. 1250-1390) and the Burjiyyah (r. 1382-1517). The Bahris were mainly Qipchaq Turks from the southern Russian steppes, while the Burjis were Chechens (or Circassians) from the northern Caucasus. As the Mamluks embraced Islam, were trained as soldiers and eventually joined the existing Mamluk hierarchy, they would be set free and would then assume Arabic names and honorific titles. They embraced and promoted orthodox Sunni Islam, and defended its holy places such as the Dome of the Rock in Jerusalem and the two great mosques in Makkah and Madinah. Most notably, the Mamluk Sultan Qutuz defeated the Mongols at the battle of 'Ayn Jalut (lit. Goliath's Spring) in 1260 in Palestine (*see page 81*) and other sultans recaptured up the Crusader strongholds at Acre, Sidon, Beirut, Haifa, and Cyprus.

Al-Mustansir
1261-1262 CE/659-661 AH
Al-Hakim I
1262-1302 CE/661-701 AH
Al-Mustakfi I
1302-1340 CE/701-740 AH
Al-Wathiq I
1340-1341 CE/740-741 AH
Al-Hakim II
1341-1352 CE/741-753 AH

Al-Mu'tadid I
1352-1362 CE/753-763 AH
Al-Mutawakkil I
(2nd time) 1362-1377 CE/763-779 AH
Al-Mu'tasim
(1st time)1377 CE/779 AH
Al-Mutawakkil I
(2nd time)1377-1383 CE/779-785 AH
Al-Wathiq II
1383-1386 CE/785-788 AH

Al-Mu'tasim
(2nd time)1386-1389 CE/788-791 AH
Al-Mutawakkil I
(3rd time) 1389-1406 CE/791-808 AH
Al-Musta'in
1406-1414 CE/808-816 AH
Al-Mu'tadid II
1414-1441 CE/816-845 AH
Al-Mustakfi II
1441-1451 CE/845-855 AH

Al-Qa'im
1451-1455 CE/855-859 AH
Al-Mustanjid
1455-1479 CE/859-884 AH
Al-Mutawakkil II
1479-1497 CE/884-903 AH
Al-Mustamsik
(1st time) 1497-1508 CE/903-914 AH
Al-Mutawakkil III
(1st time)1508-1516 CE/914-922 AH

Al-Mustamsik
(2nd time)1516-1517 CE/922-923 AH
Al-Mutawakkil III
(2nd time) 1517 CE/923 AH
(Ottoman invasion of Eygpt)

Shadow 'Abbasid Caliphate
(under Mamluk patronage in Cairo)

The Mamluks, 1250-1517

THE MAMLUKS

1250CE 648AH

The Mamluks capture Egypt and Syria from the Ayyubids.

1260CE 659AH

The Mamluks defeat the Mongols at the battle of Ayn Jalut.

The Mamluks built many great monuments, and supported Islamic scholars across all disciplines including Ibn Khaldun (*see page 78*), Ibn Hajar, al-'Ayni, al-Sakhawi, Jalal al-Din al-Suyuti, al-Subki, al-Safadi, Ibn Taghribirdi, al-Maqrizi and al-Qalqashandi. They brought stability and prosperity to Egypt and controlled the spice trade.

1281–1324CE 680–724AH

Reign of Uthman Ibn Ertoghrul who establishes the Ottoman dynasty.

1304–1369CE 703–770AH

Life of the great traveller Ibn Battutah.

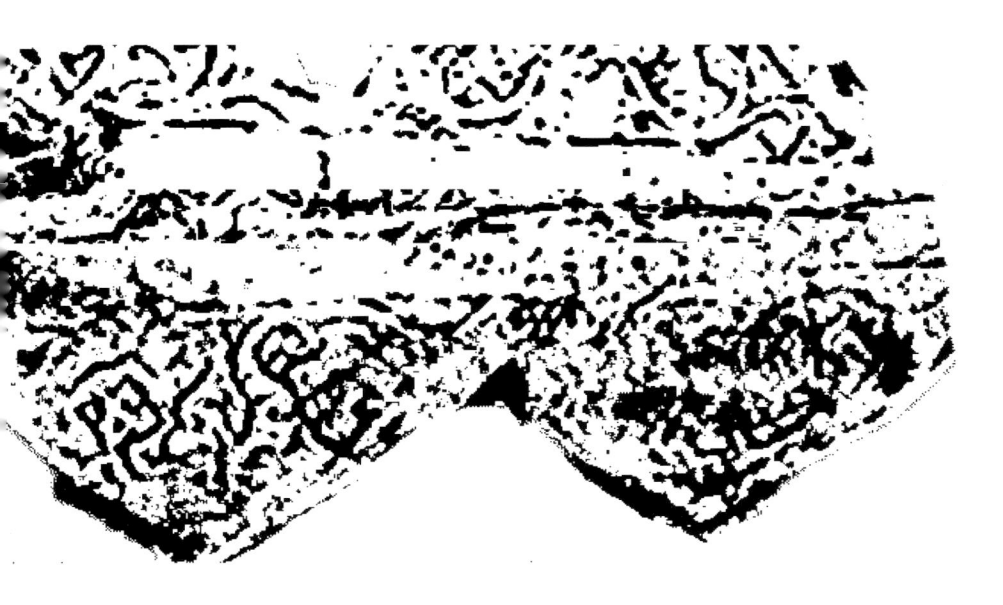

The Mamluk government or sultanate was known as the Dawlat al-Turk, and some dialects of Turkish remained their language of everyday usage. While their knowledge of Arabic was superficial, they had a powerful awareness of Islam. A prime example of this sensitivity came in June 1261 when Sultan Baybars I al-Bunduqdari installed a prince of the 'Abbasid family as the caliph of Islam with pomp and ceremony in Cairo, and received from him a formal delegation of authority as the universal sultan of Islam. The caliph assumed the regal title of al-Mustansir Billah. When this first 'Abbasid caliph of Cairo died prematurely in an ill-fated attempt to recover Baghdad from the Il-Khans (r. 1256-1353), Sultan Baybars I installed a successor, al-Hakim bi-Amrillah (r. 1262-1302), whose descendants were recognised as caliphs in Egypt, Syria and other Islamic territories until the Ottomans brought an end to Mamluk rule in 1517.

THE MAMLUKS

1370–1405CE **771–807AH**

The Turkish Muslim Tamerlane conquers the Middle East and South and Central Asia

Life of Zheng He, the Muslim admiral of the Chinese fleet

1371–1433CE **773–839AH**

1389CE **791AH**

The Ottoman defeat of the Serbs in Kosovo, establishing their rule in the Balkans

Life of the prolific encyclopaedist Al-Suyuti

1445–1505CE **849–911AH**

If repelled by the Mamluks at 'Ayn Jalut, the Mongol invasions had done much to destroy and displace the old order in the Muslim east. The ongoing migration of Turkish tribes into Anatolia and Iran during this period changed the ethnic composition of these regions.

The conversion of the Mongol Il-Khans to Islam, under Mahmud Ghazan (r. 1295-1304), and their later adoption, along with other Turkish and Mongol rulers, of Persian forms of government, language and culture, led to a greater distinction between a Persian east (Iran, Anatolia, Central Asia and India) and an Arab western cultural zone in the Muslim world. Politically these later Turkish migrations into Iran and Anatolia helped to hasten the fragmentation

Tombs of the Mamluk kings in Cairo

Expulsion of Muslims and Jews from Spain

1492CE **898AH**

The Ottoman conquest of Syria and Egypt ends the Mamluk dynasty

1517CE **923AH**

1453CE **857AH**

Mehmet II conquers Constantinople and makes it his capital, ending the Byzantine dynasty

Colourless glass basin, inlaid with lotus flowers and Naskh script which repeats the word, al-'alim ('the wise'), Egypt or Syria, fourteen century. This glassware was often exported to Europe and to the Far East.

Mamluk spherical brass incense burner of Amir Badr al-Din Baysari (d.1298), Damascus, Syria. Incense was a valued commodity of the day

of the Saljuq Empire and contributed to rise fo successor states, the most improtant of which was to be that of the Ottomans.

In the Muslim west, the last great Muslim empire to connect Europe and North Africa, that of the Almohads, fell in 1269. Thereafter, in al-Andalus, only the Nasirids of Grandada were able to forestall the Christian conquest of all of Iberia until 1492. North Africa was split between three Berber dynasties, the Hafsids of Tunis (r. 1229-1569), the 'Abdalwadids (r. 1236-1554), and the Marinids of Fez (r. 1269-1465), in a period that was mrked by political instability between the cities and their hinterlands.

THE MAMLUKS

IBN KHALDUN
THE FATHER OF SOCIOLOGY

Ibn Khaldun (1332-1406), the fourteenth-century Arab historian and historiographer, was an original thinker who is now seen as one of the founding figures of modern historiography, economics and sociology. The renowned historian Arnold Toynbee regarded Ibn Khaldun's most famous work, the *Muqaddimah*, as 'undoubtedly the greatest work of its kind that has yet been created by any mind in any time or place'. Its impact on nineteenth and twentieth-century European intellectual history has perhaps been more profound than upon currents of thought in the Muslim world, although there is evidence that the Egyptian historian al-Maqrizi and later on the Ottomans were influenced by Ibn Khaldun's theories.

Born in Tunis to a family of Yemeni origin that had migrated to al-Andalus and then North Africa, Ibn Khaldun grew up during a period of political instability that was to shape his thinking profoundly. He received an excellent education, but also suffered loss at a comparatively young age. His parents and several of his teachers died from the plague (or the Black Death) when he was only 17. During the early period of his life, Ibn Khaldun served in a number of courts in North Africa and Andalusia, but the extreme political instability meant that he was forced to move on many occasions.

The murder of his close friend, Ibn al-Khatib, the great intellectual and vizier to Muhammad ibn al-Ahmar, the ruler of Granada, in 1375 led Ibn Khaldun to retreat from public life. For four years, Ibn Khaldun composed his great work, the *Muqaddimah*, which formed the introduction to his longer universal history, *Kitab al-Ibar* (*The Book of Admonitions*), in retreat at the Castle of Ibn Salamah, near Oran in modern-day Algeria.

He then served again in various courts, and also presided a number of times as a *qadi* (judge), before finally settling down in 1382, and spending the rest of his days in Cairo, where Barquq, the Mamluk sultan, appointed him as the chief Maliki *qadi*.

In 1400, at the age of nearly 70, Ibn Khaldun was asked to mediate with the last great Mongol conqueror of the Middle East, Tamerlane (Timur) on behalf of the city of Damascus, which was then under siege from the Mongol forces. Ibn Khaldun records the meeting between one of Islam's greatest historians with a world historical figure in his Autobiography. He found Tamerlane to be 'highly intelligent and very perspicacious'; while Timur's own biographer recorded that the conqueror had returned the compliment, being impressed by Ibn Khaldun's 'distinguished appearance and handsome countenance'.

Ibn Khaldun's overriding concern in his *Muqaddimah* is to analyse in a systematic and rigorous way the reasons why nations rise and fall in power. His analysis is divided into six sections looking at the kinds of human society, nomadic societies, the various kinds of political orders, sedentary societies, kinds of economic activity and the varieties of learning and knowledge. Ibn Khaldun's method was notably empiricist as he was concerned to draw his conclusions based on observation rather than trying to reconcile his observations with preconceived ideas.

A major question he asked is still relevant today: what is social solidarity and how can a society attain and maintain it? For Ibn Khaldun, any successful society must be largely agreed upon its ultimate values and goals. This sense of social solidarity – or *'asabiyah* – was most powerful in tribal societies driven by the need for survival in difficult conditions, and the strength of the ties of kinship. Set against these poor but united nomadic peoples are the sedentary societies: these have economic power and civilisation but they lack fighting spirit and social solidarity. Ibn Khaldun observed that there was a cycle of history in which nomadic peoples conquer sedentary societies, become civilised yet decadent, and were then themselves conquered by new nomads.

Although best known for his work on social solidarity and the cyclical nature of power (*mulk*), Ibn Khaldun also had much to say about city versus country, bureaucracy versus the military, taxation, economics and education that has been widely appreciated.

Ibn Khaldun [right]

An artist's impression of Ibn Khaldun, now widely seen as the foundng father of sociology.

Tamerlane [left]

Tamerlane as depicted in 1370

THE MAMLUKS

A Mamluk Cavalier

An artist's impression

KINGDOM
OF CYPRUS

■ HOMS

TIPOLI

■ BAALBEK

MEDITERRANEAN SEA

SIDON ■

TYRE ■

ACRE ■

KINGDOM
OF JERUSALEM

■ DAMASCUS

MONGOL
FORCES

'AYN JALUT ■

MAMLUK
FORCES

■ BOSRA

■ SALT

■ JERUSALEM

HEBRON ■

Battle of 'Ayn Jalut

80   A JOURNEY THROUGH ISLAMIC HISTORY

'Ayn Jalut
DEFEAT OF THE MONGOLS

The series of Mongol invasions in the Muslim World during the eleventh century were among the most calamitous in the long annals of Islamic history. In 1258, the Mongols had sacked Baghdad, and, for all intents and purposes, ended the 'Abbasid caliphate. The Mongols then conquered Syria and besieged Damascus, forcing its surrender after a month. Hulegu, the Mongol warlord, whose warrior horde was estimated to be a third-of-a-million strong, then wrote to the Mamluks, the one Sunni power then remaining in the Middle East: 'You should think of what happened to other countries … and submit to us.'

Muzaffar Sayf al-Din Qutuz, the third Mamluk Sultan, who had been raised as a warrior, consulted with his generals, who recommended capitulation in the face of such an overwhelming military force. Yet Qutuz decided that he could not surrender without a fight, despite his 20,000-man army being outnumbered fifteen-to-one. Fate then intervened when the Great Khan, Mongke, died, and Hulegu, alongside all the other Mongol princes, was called back to select Mongke's successor. Hulegu pulled the main body of his forces back to Maraghah in Iran, but, confident of success against the Mamluks of Egypt, sent on a smaller force of 20,000 under the command of Kitbugha.

Kitbugha was then unsuccessful in getting the Crusaders to ally with him against the Mamluks. Qutuz, realising that the military situation now favoured him, abandoned his defensive preparations, and went on the offensive, succeeding in gaining the Crusaders as allies.

A small army that Qutuz sent under the command of Baybars succeeded in defeating a vanguard Mongol force near Gaza. Then, establishing his main army on the narrow part of the Plain of Esdraelon at 'Ayn Jalut, Qutuz trapped Kitbugha by the use of a ruse, making him believe that Baybars' smaller force constituted all of Mamluk Egypt's military strength. Following hard on Baybars' retreating force, Kitbugha was then outflanked and caught in a pincer movement. At one point when his flank seemed to waver, Qutuz flung his helmet onto the ground so that his troops could recognise him and rallied them, calling out 'O Muslims!' three times. Kitbugha was then captured under the renewed Mamluk assault, taken to Qutuz and then executed. Leaderless, the Mongol army fled, and in a matter of days the Mamluks recaptured Aleppo and the other major Syrian cities, entering Damascus in triumph.

The victory at 'Ayn Jalut marked one of the great turning points in history. Had the Mongols won there, they might have carried all of North Africa and gone on to threaten Europe from the south and the east. Instead, Qutuz's victory left the Mamluks as the pre-eminent Sunni power for 200 years before the rise of the Ottomans, and marked the beginning of the end for the tenuous Crusader presence in the Middle East. But, most importantly, it broke the Mongol reputation for invincibility, for their defeat at 'Ayn Jalut signalled the end of any serious attempt on their part to capture Egypt and the Levant.

For Qutuz, however, there was to be no personal triumph for he was shortly murdered thereafter by his ambitious deputy, Baybars, who rode back in triumph in his stead through the gates of Cairo.

The Ottomans
Safavids and Mughals

907-1342 AH
1501-1924 CE

In the period between 1453 and 1526, three major Muslim empires emerged that once again centralised political power after the fragmentation of the 'Abbasid caliphate in the late tenth century. Stretching from the western borders of Morocco to the Bay of Bengal and together controlling a population of between 130-160 million, these were the Ottomans in the Mediterranean world, the Safavids in Iran and the Mughals of India. Combining military prowess, cultural sophistication, aesthetic magnificence and economic wealth, these three empires represented the last great expressions of Muslim political power, a power that was decisively broken with the emergence of European colonialism in the Muslim world from the eighteenth century onwards.

The Ottomans (c.1281-1922)

Sulayman the Magnificent (r.1520-1566)

The Ottoman Turks created the most enduring and expansive of the three great empires – the Ottomans, the Safavids and the Mughals – of the final third of Islamic history. In the late thirteenth century, 'Uthman I (r. c.1281-1324), so the story is told, had a dream of a great tree growing from his navel that would provide shade for the mountains. A holy man, Edebali, interpreted 'Uthman's dream to mean that he would found a great empire. In control of a small frontier warrior (*ghazi*) state in Bursa, Western Anatolia, 'Uthman and his successors worked to realise his dream. During the fourteenth and fifteenth centuries, the Ottomans captured much of Anatolia and South-east Europe. Despite a defeat at the Battle of Ankara in 1402 at the hands of Tamerlane they were able to regroup, re-conquer and continue their military expansion. The Ottomans crossed into Europe in 1357 and began to expand their power in the Balkans. They captured Sophia in Bulgaria in 1385, defeated the King of Hungary at the battle of Nicopolis in 1396, conquered Thessalonica and Macedonia in 1430, and occupied Albania in 1435-36.

The Ottomans

Bayezid II
1481-1512 CE/886-918 AH
Selim I ('the Grim')
1512-1520 CE/918-926 AH
Suleyman II ('Law-giver'/'Magnificent')
1520-1566 CE/926-974 AH
Selim II
1566-1574 CE/974-982 AH
Murad III
1574-1595 CE/982-1003 AH
Muhammad III
1595-1603 CE/1003-1012 AH

Ahmed I
1603-1617 CE/1012-1026 AH
Mustafa I (first reign)
1617-1618 CE/1026-1027 AH
'Uthman II
1618-1622 CE/1027-1031 AH
Mustafa I (second reign)
1622-1623 CE/1031-1032 AH
Murad IV
1623-1640 CE/1032-1049 AH

Ibrahim
1640-1648 CE/1049-1058 AH
Muhammad IV
1648-1687 CE/1058-1099 AH
Suleyman III
1687-1691 CE/1099-1102 AH
Ahmed II
1691-1695 CE/1102-1106 AH
Mustafa II
1695-1703 CE/1106-1115 AH

Ahmed III
1703-1730 CE/1115-1143 AH
Mahmud I
1730-1754 CE/1143-1168 AH
'Uthman III
1754-1757 CE/1168-1171 AH
Mustafa III
1757-1774 CE/1171-1187 AH
Abdulhamid I
1774-1789 CE/1187-1203 AH

Selim III
1789-1807 CE/1203-1222 AH
Mustafa IV
1807-1808 CE/1222-1223 AH
Mahmud II
1808-1839 CE/1223-1255 AH
Abdulmecid I
1839-1861 CE/1255-1277 AH
Abdulaziz
1861-1876 CE/1277-1293 AH

Murad V
1876 CE/1293 AH
Abdulhamid II
1876-1909 CE/1293-1327 AH
Muhammad V Reshad
1909-1918 CE/1327-1336 AH
Muhammad VI Wahdeddin (last sultan)
1839-1861 CE/1255-1277 AH
Abdulmecid II (as caliph only)
1922-1924 CE/1341-1342 AH

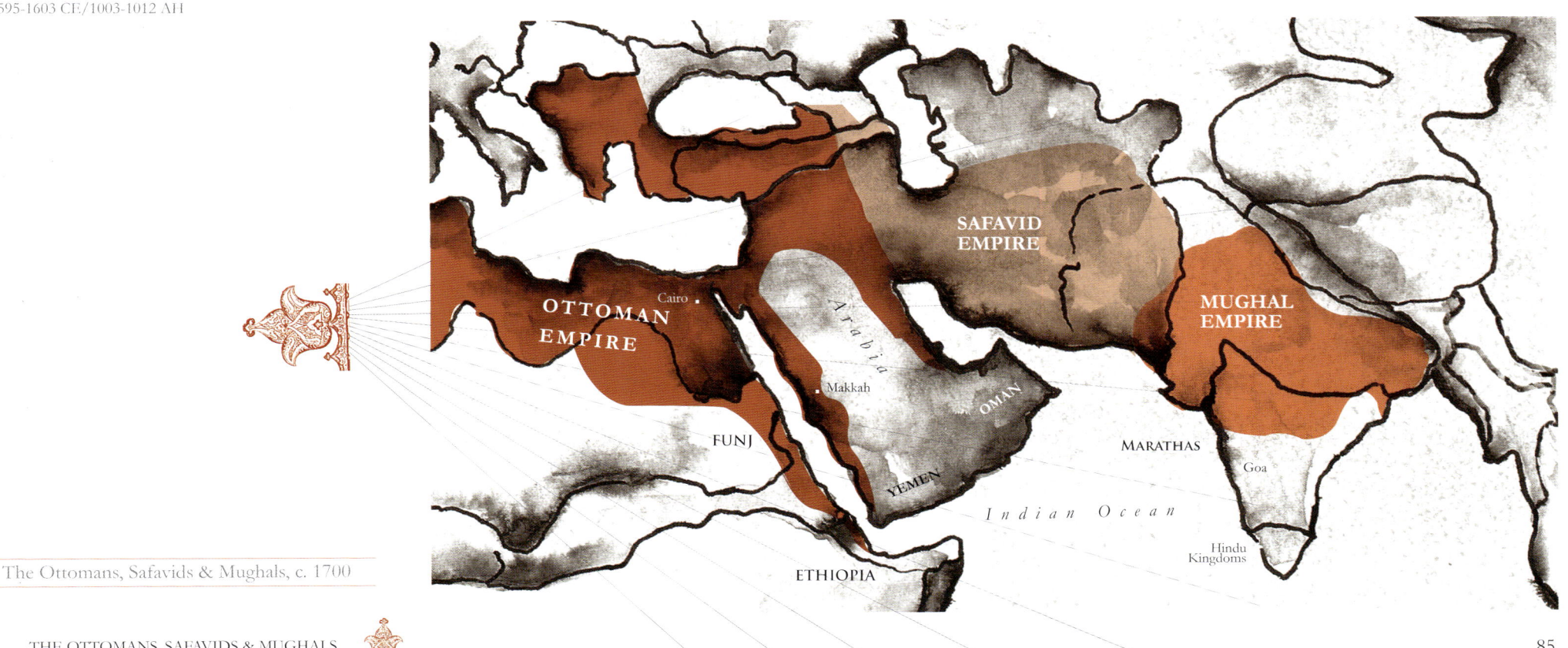

The Ottomans, Safavids & Mughals, c. 1700

THE OTTOMANS, SAFAVIDS & MUGHALS

Sinan
The Great Architect

The works of Sinan, the legendary architect of the Ottoman Sultans, served not only to standardise but to define the classic appearance of Ottoman architecture in its mosques, *madrasah*s, fountains and other public works, and represents one of the most influential strands in Islamic architecture overall. Sinan was born as a *devshirme*, or a Christian conscript in the Ottoman army. As a young man, Sinan was trained in architecture and engineering during the reign of Selim I, and, in his early career, was involved in logistical support during military campaigns, constructing or restoring bridges, stores, warehouses and waterworks. Sinan's talent was recognised and he was promoted several times, before being finally appointed as the chief architect to the Ottoman Sultans. Even in Sinan's day, architects were not only master builders but were also in charge of regulating urban development, for instance, implementing a ban on the construction of tall buildings in Sultanahmet Square to protect the ancient Byzantine cisterns that lay underneath, which lasted up until the nineteenth century.

The exact number of Sinan's works is disputed, but over two hundred that have survived are recognised as being his. Of his masterpieces, which are many in number, one of the greatest is the Sulemaniye Complex built between 1550-1557, commissioned, as its name suggests, by Suleyman the 'Lawgiver' as he is remembered by the Turks (r. 1520-1566). Set on a slope overlooking the Golden Horn, the complex was terraced to provide space for a grand congregational mosque, two mausoleums, six madrasahs, a Qur'an school, a hostel, a hospital, a caravanserai, a bath, a public kitchen and many small shops. The documents concerning the construction of the complex reveal that half the 3500 builders were Christian, and that on completion it employed over 700 people.

Sultanahmed Mosque, Istanbul, interior

The mosque itself is a monumental mass of domes, surrounded by four thin minarets. As with his other designs, Sinan based the design of the mosque on the great Byzantine church Hagia Sophia, but succeeded in opening up the nave and aisles to form a single space more suitable to the ranks of the congregational prayer through the use of four columns to support the massive dome. Unlike the small mosque that Sinan built for the vizier Rustem Pasha, the use of coloured *iznik* tiles is very restrained in the Sulemaniye.

Among its architectural ingenuities was an air filter designed to prevent air pollution from candle soot, and collected it for reuse as ink employed to protect manuscripts from being damaged by insects and worms.

As chief architect, Sinan served under three successive sultans until his death in 1588, yet, despite leaving behind many architectural marvels, he designed his own charming tomb to be small and unassuming.

Sinan's Selimiye at Edirne

1501–1524CE **907–930AH**

Reign of Shah Isma'il I, founder of the Safavid dynasty

1520–1566CE **926–972AH**

Reign of Suleyman II, the greatest of the Ottoman sultans

In 1453, Mehmed II the Conqueror (r. 1451-1481), finally captured Constantinople, ending the Byzantine Empire, the last manifestation of the ancient Eastern Roman Empire that had endured for over a millennium since its founding by Constantine I in 330. Mehmed annexed Serbia in 1459 and took the southern Crimea in 1475. After 1500, Selim I (r. 1512-1520) doubled the size of the empire by conquering Syria and Egypt, ending the Mamluk dynasty in the process as well as taking control of the Hijaz and Algeria. The last 'Abbasid shadow-caliph, Mutawakil III, was brought to Istanbul in 1517, but it is doubtful whether the Ottomans made a full and lasting claim to be the true successors of the 'Abbasids.

Sultan Mehmed II al-Fatih

Conqueror of Constantinople in 1453

Selim I the Grim

Reign of Babur, founder
of the Mughal dynasty

1526–1530CE **933–937AH**

Reign of Akbar, the most
powerful Mughal emperor

1556–1605CE **963–1014AH**

The Hijaz Railway

Built by Sultan 'Abdulhamid II

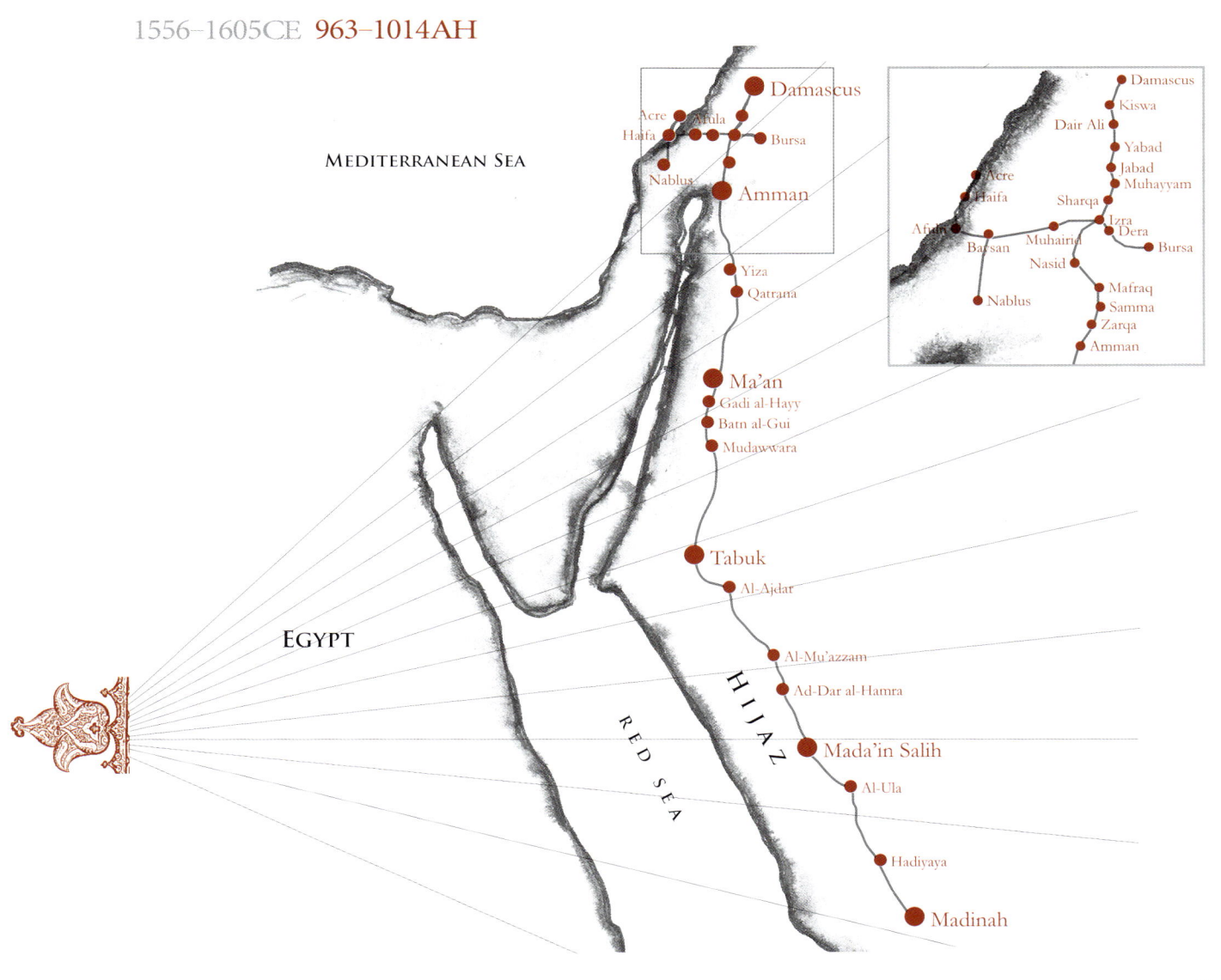

THE OTTOMANS, SAFAVIDS & MUGHALS

89

THE JANISSARIES

A Janissary

A portrait by Gentile Bellini
(c.1429-1507)

The Janissaries, from the Turkish *yeni cheri*, meaning 'new force', were an elite infantry order within the Ottoman Empire based on *devshirme*, the Ottoman system of military conscription. The main feature of *devshirme* was taking Christian boys, mostly from Ottoman provinces in the Balkans, converting them to Islam, and training them to serve in the elite ranks of the Ottoman army, although not exclusively so. The formation of the Janissaries may be dated back to as early as 1330, and it was further developed in Murad II's second reign (r. 1446-1451) and became fully organised under Selim I (r. 1512-1520). It served the Ottoman army for nearly 500 years; its soldiers performed outstandingly even though it remained a minor division within the Ottoman army. The Janissaries were put down and broken up by Mahmut II in 1826 when they opposed the creation of a new regular corps, the Muallem Eshkinji ('drilled guard').

Traditionally the Turks had fought as mounted cavalry, but increasingly realised the need to develop their infantry. The early conversion to Islam of the conscripted Janissaries was found to be highly effective in ensuring their loyalty to the cause of the Ottoman Empire. The Janissaries were originally prohibited from marrying, but in 1581 this prohibition was relaxed; thereafter, membership became increasingly hereditary which blunted the effectiveness of the Janissaries, whose selection had previously been based solely upon military prowess. They also became at times a very powerful political block within the empire, not only determining the choice of the sultan's chief minister, the vizier, but even at times successfully demanding huge bribes before allowing a new sultan to ascend to the throne. They were often appointed as provincial military governors (*aga*s) as well.

Conscription under the *devshirme* system focused on Christian boys from rural villages; yet the Ottoman records show that Muslims from rural locales were not entirely excluded either. Jews were excluded but not for reasons of anti-Semitism; but because Jewish populations were largely urban and it was felt that a rural background was more amenable to shaping a loyal corps. The levy was held every few years, and with restrictions (e.g. recruiting between the ages of 10 and 12, and not from families with only one son),

The Turkish Sultan reviewing his Janissaries
French School, 18th century, engraving

and usually under the rubric of the tacit consent of the villages where the levy took place. Often, for very poor families, conscription was rightly seen as an advantageous route into wealth and power, and competition for places was not unknown. Generally speaking the numbers taken in any one year were a few thousand, and anti-Ottoman sources have tended to exaggerate the scale of the levy.

The education of the boys was organised according to aptitude, and the more academically inclined were trained at an elite school within the royal palace itself, the Enderun, to become the administrators, engineers and *mufti*s of the empire as well as cavalrymen, officers and generals. Life at the Enderun was disciplined, exacting and committed to the highest standards in education and etiquette: these boys from the poor remote villages of the Caucasus and the Balkans were schooled to run an empire.

Some of the most famous graduates included the grand viziers who ran the empire like Sokulla Mehmet Pasha and Mahmud Pasha, the master architect Sinan, and many gifted musicians like Ali Ufki Bey, calligraphers, litterateurs, and leading jurists, judges and Islamic scholars. Similarly girls were also part of *devshirme*, with the vast majority marrying into the aristocratic elite, which was defined legally and socially rather than through hereditary status. As an institution, *devshirme* began to decline in the seventeenth century and practically ceased to exist by the mid-eighteenth century when the recruitment of Muslim Turks became predominant.

1560CE 968AH

The Ottoman empire reaches its greatest size

1571–1640CE 979–1050AH

Life of Mulla Sadra, the great Persian philosopher

1587–1629CE 955–1038AH

Reign of Shah 'Abbas, the greatest Safavid ruler

Suleyman I the Magnificent (or 'the Legislator') (r. 1520-1566) secured further territorial expansion. His navy secured the command of the Red Sea and the Yemen and the increasing dominance of the Mediterranean, underscored by the capture of the North African coast and Malta. Among Suleyman's greatest admirals were Hayrettin Barbarosa and Piri Reis. His armies pushed forward into Europe with the capture of a huge swathe of territory stretching from the Dalmatian coast through Hungary and Moldova to the Crimea, and an unsuccessful first siege of Vienna in 1529. A lasting legacy of the Ottomans was the spread of Islam in the Balkans, notably among the peoples of Bosnia, Kosovo and Albania.

Suleyman also set out the classic form of Ottoman rule, the most sophisticated pre-modern form of government, whose subjects, Muslim and non-Muslim, provided the wealth that supported the military and state apparatus; a system effective enough to survive as a great power despite European expansion up to the mid-nineteenth century when European-style reforms became necessary. A feuding Turkoman aristocracy was gradually replaced by the *devshirme*, an elite Christian slave class, who were exclusively loyal to the sultan. Educated from a young age and converted to Islam, they provided the elite military force, the Janissaries, with 30,000 men in Suleyman's time, and, increasingly, made up the administrative class (*see page 90*). The religious scholars (ulema) were integrated into a complicated regional hierarchy that administered religious law according to the Hanafi school, although parts of the Arab territories were exempted, who in return provided legitimacy to the sultan's rule and his independent right to issue administrative decrees; non-Muslims were organised into separate religious community (*millet*) as protected peoples (*dhimmah*).

1609–1616CE **1018–1025AH**

Construction of the
Blue Mosque in Istanbul

1628–1658CE **1037–1068AH**

Reign of the Moghul emperor, Shah
Jahan, who built the Taj Mahal

1658–1707CE **1069–1118AH**

Reign of Awrangzeb, the
last great Moghul emperor

Mosque Lamp, Iznik

Turkey, c.1510

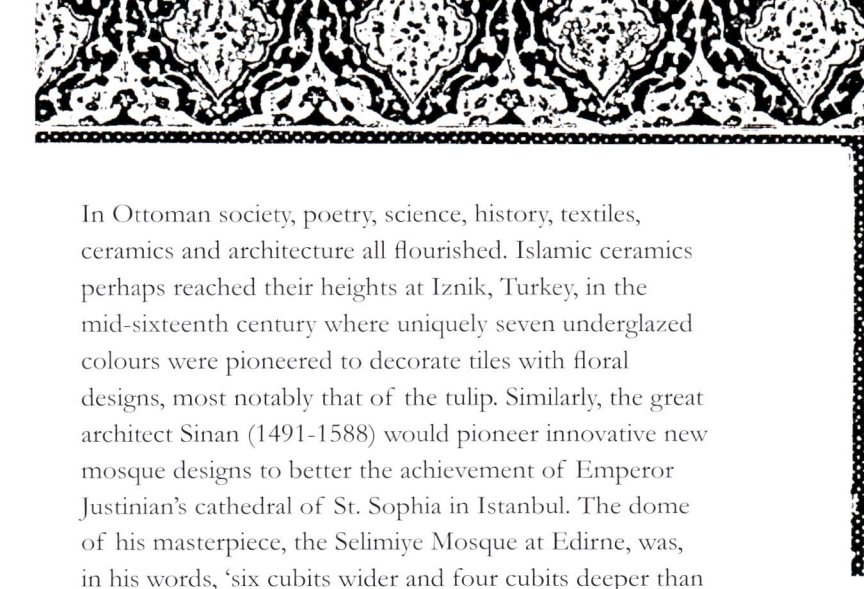

In Ottoman society, poetry, science, history, textiles, ceramics and architecture all flourished. Islamic ceramics perhaps reached their heights at Iznik, Turkey, in the mid-sixteenth century where uniquely seven underglazed colours were pioneered to decorate tiles with floral designs, most notably that of the tulip. Similarly, the great architect Sinan (1491-1588) would pioneer innovative new mosque designs to better the achievement of Emperor Justinian's cathedral of St. Sophia in Istanbul. The dome of his masterpiece, the Selimiye Mosque at Edirne, was, in his words, 'six cubits wider and four cubits deeper than the dome of St Sophia' (*see page 86*).

THE OTTOMANS, SAFAVIDS & MUGHALS

1683CE **1094AH**

The second unsuccessful
Ottoman siege of Vienna

1703–1792CE **1115–1206AH**

Life of the religious reformer
Ibn 'Abd al-Wahhab

1722–1773CE **1135–1187AH**

The final period of
Safavid rule in Persia

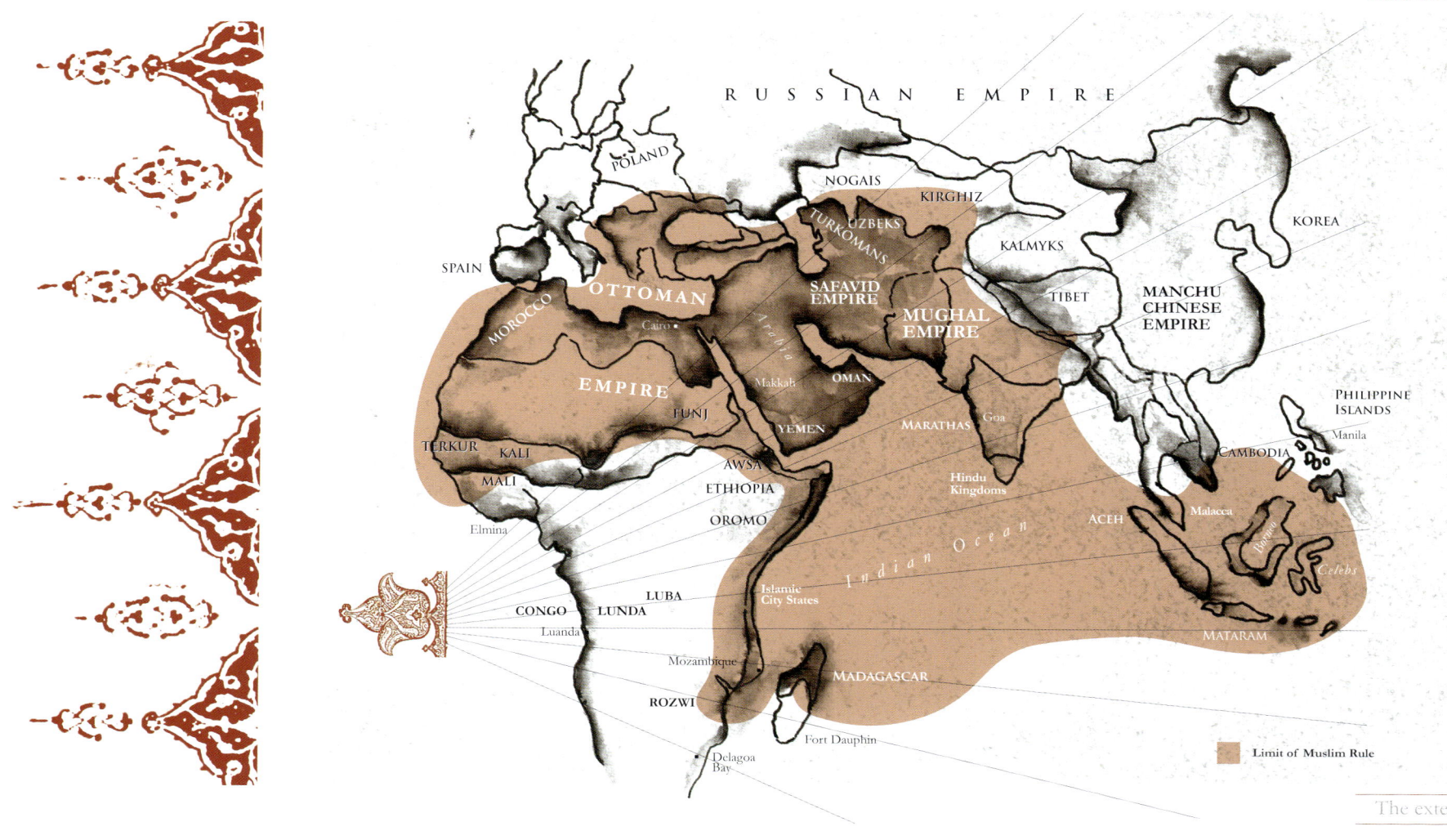

The extent of Muslim rule, c.1700

Reign of Nadir Shah, founder of the Afsharid dynasty

1736–1747CE 1149–1160AH

1754–1815CE 1167–1232AH

Life of Usman dan Fodio, founder of the Sokoto caliphate in West Africa

By the late seventeenth century that Ottoman power had begun to decline in Europe, symbolised by the Turks' final repulsion from the walls of Vienna in 1683. Their centralised military system had reached its limits, and the outlaying provinces could not be held against serious opposition, while the state system that relied on military expansion also declined. More importantly, the Ottomans could not compete with the European colonial and economic expansion, weakening their state and society, and, once both feared and admired, they were now dubbed 'the Sick Man of Europe'. In the nineteenth century, Western-style reforms were made – a conscript army, a modern education system, the adoption of French legal codes – towards a more centralised secular government, despite Abdulhamid II's reclaiming of the caliphate. Yet, territorial losses accelerated through the nineteenth and early twentieth centuries as Britain, France and Russia carved up the Ottoman legacy or nationalist movements sought independence. The Turks, after siding with Germany, were defeated by the Allied Powers during the First World War. Pinned back to their Anatolian heartland, the successors to the last great Muslim power turned to nationalism and established the secular republic of Turkey in 1924.

1798–1799CE **1213–1214AH**

Napoleon invades Egypt

The Ottomans cede territories to the Russians

1774CE **1187AH**

1805CE **1220AH**

Muhammad Ali becomes the Ottoman governor of Egypt, gaining independence later on

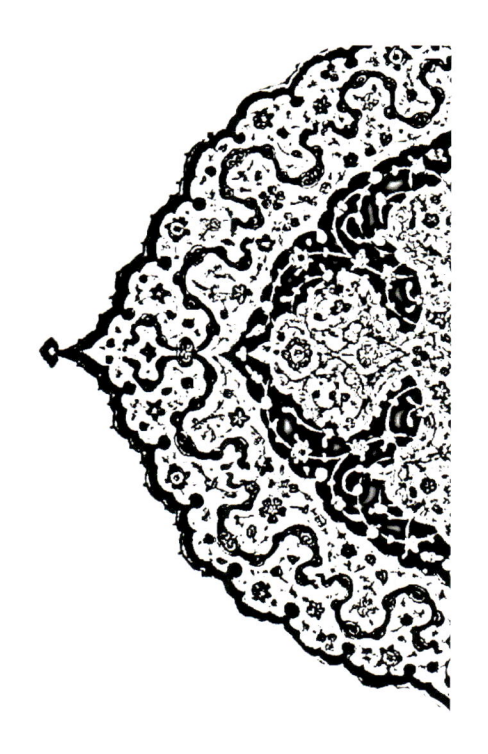

THE SAFAVIDS (1501-1722)

Obscurity surrounds the origins of the second great empire of this period, that of the Safavids, a Turkic dynasty. The ancestors of the Safavid rulers once headed the Safavid Sufi order based in Ardabil in Azerbaijan. Before their rise to power, Persia was a Sunni Muslim country, but the Safavids' main legacy was to transform Persia by making Twelver Shi'ism the test of loyalty to the state. The Safavid Shahs in the sixteenth and seventeenth centuries made the claim that they were incarnations of the hidden twelfth Imam, and mobilised Shi'i religious scholars as an instrument to strengthen state power. The pro-Shi'i foreign policy of the Safavids stretched as far as eastern Afghanistan, where Sunni Afghans took up arms to combat it.

Shah Isma'il I (r. 1501-1524), the founder of the dynasty, with the help of his Qizilbash (literally 'Red Head') supporters, who later made up the military elite, defeated the Aq Quyunlu dynasty and seized power in Azerbaijan in 1501 and then gradually brought the whole of Persia under his control.

In 1510, he defeated the Shaybanid Ozbeks near Merv, in Central Asia. but in 1514, the Ottoman Sultan Selim I defeated Shah Isma'il at Chaldiran in southern Azerbaijan, in which the superior Turkish canons bested the more primitive weapons of the Safavid Qizilbash. The Ottomans then went on to capture Diyar Bakr, Kurdistan and Baghdad – forcing the Safavids to relocate their capital from Tabriz to Qazwin under Shah Tahmasp I and then, under Shah 'Abbas I, the capital was relocated again to Isfahan.

1821–1829CE 1237–1245AH

Greek war of independence against Ottoman rule

1839–1876CE 1255–1293AH

Modernizing Tanzimat Reforms of the Ottoman Empire

When Shah Isma'il died in 1524, his ten-year old son Shah Tahmasp (r. 1524-1576) reigned for over fifty years. He had greater success than his father in converting the Sunni Persians to Twelver (Ithna 'Ashari) Shi'ism. The fifth Safavid ruler, Shah 'Abbas I (r. 1587-1629), made his dynasty most powerful in the region. He reformed the army by recruiting bodyguards from Turkish tribes known as the Shah-seven or 'those who love the King', destroying the power of the Qizilbash in 1596. Shah 'Abbas I acquired superior artillery and trained his troops in the European manner. His powerful fleet in the Persian Gulf served to enhance his prestige. Later, in 1722, the Ghilzai Afghans invaded Persia and Nadir Shah and his successors kept a series of Safavid puppets on the throne until 1773. The eighteenth century saw military conflict between two rivals, the Turkish Afshar dynasty (r. 1736-1795) and the Afghan Zand dynasty (r. 1750-1794), that inherited a partitioned Safavid Empire. Under the despotic Qajars (r. 1779-1924), Iran regained a more important position of power, notably as an ally of the European powers that sought further control of a declining Ottoman Empire.

Shah Isma'il I (r.1501-1524)
Founder of the Safavid dynasty

Shah 'Abbas I (r.1587-1629)
Patron of the arts and founder of Isfahan

THE OTTOMANS, SAFAVIDS & MUGHALS

Construction of the Suez Canal

1854–1869CE **1271–1287AH**

The Safavids were great supporters of the arts and during their time: Persian painting, carpets, textiles, ceramics and architecture reached heights of great accomplishment. Shah 'Abbas as a great patron of the arts bore comparison with his contemporaries Akbar the Great of Hindustan, Suleyman the Magnificent in Istanbul and Queen Elizabeth I of England. He succeeded in creating a textile industry, whose silks, damasks, velvets and brocades were exported to Europe; 300 Chinese potters were similarly recruited to enhance the export of ceramics. At his new capital of Isfahan, Shah 'Abbas created one of the largest and most beautiful cities of the time; a population of one million was serviced by mosques, madrasahs, caravanserais, parks and public baths. The great public square, the Maidan, represents the cream of Persian architecture with the Ali Qapu Palace and the Lutf Allah and Royal Mosques, famously decorated with the intricate tiling of the region.

Chess players, page from an early Safavid treatise on chess

Persian School, late 16th century, ink on paper

1876–1909CE 1293–1326AH

Reign of the Ottoman sultan 'Abdulhamid II, who pursues a policy of pan-Islamism

1909CE 1327AH

The Young Turks Revolution overthrows 'Abdulhamid II

Ali Qapu Palace, Isfahan

Entrance to the Lutf Allah Mosque, Isfahan

1915–1923CE **1334–1349AH**

The Armenian Genocide led by the Young Turks

THE MUGHALS (1526-1858)

Alongside the Safavids and the Ottomans, the third great empire of the age was that of the Mughal dynasty of India (or Hindustan). Muhammad Zahir al-Din Babur, a Chaghatay Turk of Central Asia and a descendant of Tamerlane and Genghis (Chinghiz) Khan, captured Kabul in 1514 and won the first battle of Panipat against the Delhi sultan Ibrahim Lodi in 1526, thereby putting an end to the Delhi Sultanate. As Emperor (Padishah) Babur (r. 1526-30) laid the foundations of the Mughal Empire in India, but his son and successor, Humayun (r. 1530-40, 1555-56) was displaced for fifteen years by a military adventurer, Sher Shah Suri, before regaining his throne. His son Akbar ruled India for a long time (r. 1556-1605) and re-established the Mughal dynasty, putting it on a firm political, military and administrative footing; its territories grew to a great extent, capturing Baluchistan, Sind, Gujarat, Bengal, Assam, Kashmir and Central India. He developed an efficient and largely fair system of tax collection right down to the village level, and laid the foundation of a governmental structure to include diverse ethnic elements, comprising Afghans, Turks, Hindus and Persians. He created an inclusive political philosophy that informed the policies of his successors, Jahangir (r. 1605-27) and Shah Jahan (r. 1628-1658), under whom India prospered and became a great power. However, Akbar's attempt at an eclectic new religion (*din-i ilahi*) for his courtly elite proved unacceptable to the orthodox Sunni religious scholars.

Akbar, the young king and falconer

1922–1924CE 1341–42AH

Turkey establishes its modern borders and abolishes the Ottoman sultanate and the caliphate

1932CE 1351AH

Establishment of Saudi Arabia and independence of Iraq

During the reign of Emperor Awrangzeb (r. 1658-1707) Mughal power reached its peak, and most of southern India was conquered. Personally pious and ascetic by temperament, Awrangzeb promoted Islamic orthodoxy and his reign produced some legal documents known as *Fatawa-i Alamgiri*. However, this promotion was at the cost of alienating many of his non-Muslim subjects, Hindus and Sikhs among them. His conquests in the Deccan also kept Awrangzeb away from North India in the later part of his reign, the result of which was that sections of the Indian nobility, like the Marathas, gained greater independence.

The Mughals ruled for another century and a half, during which their power declined both politically and economically. In the wake of the Industrial Revolution in Europe, the English East India Company looked for trading opportunities in Asia, and gained a foothold in Bengal after the battle of Plassey in 1757. The East India Company, alongside other European powers, not only gained market concessions for its industrial products but through gaining tax concessions, they eventually built an empire. After the Sepoy Uprising (by British Indian soldiers) of 1857, the British attacked Delhi and put an end to the Mughal Empire, crowning Victoria Empress of India and placing it under direct British rule in 1858.

Akbar tiger hunting near Nawar, Gwalior

From the *Akbarnama*, made for Akbar by Abul Fazl, gouache on parchment, 1590-98

Babar (r.r. 1526-30)

Founder of the Mughal dynasty

THE OTTOMANS, SAFAVIDS & MUGHALS

The Mughals were great patrons of the arts – Persian and later Urdu flourished as literary languages, and there were notable achievements in painting and architecture. Akbar, learned but illiterate, the first great patron of painters, had amassed 24,4000 illustrated manuscripts in his personal library by the time of his death. At the royal studio, Persian and Hindu literary classics as well as the great epics of the Mughal House were lavishly illustrated. The Mughal painting tradition became more realist and concerned to depict individual human emotion, as can be seen in the work of Mansur.

Zebra, from the "Minto Album", Mughal, 1621

Attributed to the great artist Mansur in the Emperor Jahangir's own hand

Akbar's imperial city Fatehpur-Sikri married Muslim arches, domes and courts with Hindu ornamentation and flat stone beams. Even grander were Shah Jahan's imperial city at Shahjahanabad, the vast Red Fort at Lahore and the peerless Taj Mahal, built to hold his beloved queen, Mumtaz Mahal, a poem in stone to marital love (*see page 104*). The walled Mughal gardens were reflections of the gardens of Paradise – the inscription to Akbar's garden tomb at Sikandra read, 'These are the gardens of Eden, enter them to dwell therein eternally.'

Fatepuri Sikri

Akbar's imnperial city, which reflected classic Islamic and indigenous Indian styles of architecture and ornamentation

The Emperor Jahangir

Preferring the company of Sufis to kings

THE OTTOMANS, SAFAVIDS & MUGHALS

THE TAJ MAHAL
THE SYMBOL OF LOVE

Shah Jahan (r. 1628-1666) ruled over the vast Mughal Empire at the height of its power and magnificence, but he is best remembered for the Taj Mahal, the masterpiece of Mughal architecture and a universal symbol of love, dedicated to the memory of his beloved wife, Mumtaz Mahal, or 'the Chosen One of the Palace'.

Shah Jahan was brought up within the household of his grandfather, Akbar the Great, and was raised to rule. He soon showed himself to be a talented administrator and soldier. On ascending to the throne, he worked to promote the major Muslim festivals and the Hajj, to extend the boundaries of the empire (although he made little headway against the Safavids in the north-east), and to improve imperial administration. The huge annual income of the Emperor amounted to some 31 million rupees, which not only funded his military campaigns but also the extensive patronage of the arts and architecture. One sign of his wealth and ostentation was the construction of the Peacock Throne, made with 8.6 million rupees in jewels and 1.4 million rupees in gold, and every part of which was encrusted in diamonds, rubies, emeralds and pearls. Yet Shah Jahan also renovated the shrine of Mu'in al-Din Chishti at Ajmer, adding a Friday mosque, pavilions and gardens.

Of his wives, Shah Jahan's favourite was Mumtaz Mahal, upon whom he centred 'his whole delight', according to one contemporary witness, and 'the mutual affection and harmony between the two had reached a degree never seen between a husband and wife among the classes of the rulers'. They married when he was 20 and she was 19, and she bore him 14 children, of whom seven survived, including four princes. In 1631, however, Mumtaz died in childbirth and the emperor fell into grief and despair, such that his constant weeping forced him to wear spectacles and one-third of his beard and moustache turned white in a matter of days.

Inspired by a verse written for her funeral – 'May the abode of Mumtaz Mahal be paradise' – Shah Jahan decided to

Mumtaz Mahal

The Taj Mahal

built a great monument, known at the time as 'the illumined tomb', as a mausoleum for his beloved, which took 17 years to build. The best stonecutters and bricklayers, stonecarvers and craftsmen in stone inlay were hired from all over the empire, and the mausoleum complex was constructed variously of fired bricks, sandstone from Agra, white marble from Rajasthan, and polished plaster. While two notable architects – Ustadh Ahmad Lahauri and Mir 'Abdul Karim – are associated with the Taj Mahal, Shah Jahan remained the driving force behind the whole conceptual design of the complex, which he oversaw annually on the anniversary of his wife's death.

Standing on the banks of the River Jumna, the Taj Mahal was conceived as an allegory of the Day of Resurrection, designed to be an earthly reflection of the afterlife. The four water channels of the gardens reflected the four paradisal rivers; the marble platform where they meet, the pool of abundance, al-Kawthar. The mausoleum itself was meant to represent the Throne from which judgement would be dispensed on the Day of Reckoning, and the four minarets, the supports of the Throne. To underscore this, the four arches are inscribed with verses from Surah Yasin which describe the events of Judgement Day. As Qazwini, Shah Jahan's historian noted, the emperor intended the Taj to be 'a masterpiece for ages to come' for the 'amazement of all humanity'.

Shah Jahan

The Rise of European Power

1214-1342 AH
1800-1924 CE

If, in the mid-sixteenth century, the Muslim world and the European powers were equally matched, by 1800, the balance of power had shifted towards Europe due to her scientific and industrial revolutions. The French Emperor Napoleon's short-lived invasion of Egypt in 1798 was not halted by the Muslims but by the British navy. European military power was able to colonise or penetrate the Muslim world allowing European manufacturing to undercut traditional Muslim producers with cheap mass-produced goods leading to economic decline. The British (Middle East, South and South-East Asia), the French (North and West Africa, Syria and Indochina), the Dutch (South-East Asia) and the Russians (Central Asia) along with others were able to build considerable global empires including in large parts of the Muslim world.

After a long presence the British were recognised as supreme in India by 1818 and forty years later imposed direct rule. Britain then extended its power to both shores of the Arabian Gulf, and, after the construction of the Suez Canal in 1869, succeeded, after a struggle with France, in controlling Egypt in 1882 and then the Sudan in 1898. In the 1870s they began to spread their empire to the Malay princely states and to Nigeria after 1914.

Throughout the eighteenth and nineteenth centuries the Russians advanced southwards into the Muslim world at the expense of

The British take possession of Aden, 1879

Illustration from Hutchinson's Story of the British Nation, an example of popular imperial propaganda, c.1923, lithograph

the Ottoman Empire and the Central Asian Khanates taking Crimea, Daghistan, Azerbaijan, Kazakhstan, Turkestan, Turkmenia and Bukhara between 1783 and 1895. The French and Russian Empires, unlike the British, created significant colonies for European settlers. In the French case their main colonies were Algeria (1830) and Tunisia (1881) from which they went on to seize nearly all of Sub-Saharan West Africa up to 1914. After 1800, the Dutch government took over from its East India Company and over time gained control of the entire South-East Asian archipelago at the end of the war of Aceh in 1908.

The flag of the British East India Company

Napoleon invades Egypt in 1798

By 1900, nine European empires, along with the Chinese, ruled over 80% of the *ummah*; only about 20% of Muslims lived in the remaining independent Muslim states – the Ottoman Empire, Persia, the Arabian Peninsula, Morocco and Afghanistan. In the early twentieth century, these remaining territories were either carved up, made into European protectorates or were subjected to significant external controls. The chief victim of this final period was the now-diminished Ottoman Empire, the only remaining great Muslim power. The European powers successfully used their influence to support various Christian peoples of the Balkans – the Greeks, Serbians, Romanians and Bulgarians – to throw off Ottoman rule, leaving only Macedonia, Thrace and Constantinople as Turkish possessions. Britain and France signed a secret treaty called Sykes-Picot Agreement on 16th May 1916 during World War I; the purpose of the agreement was to dismember the Ottoman Empire and to partition its provinces between Britain and France. It was largely the British who encouraged the Arab independence movements against the Turks. In 1917, the British issued the Balfour Declaration in support of a Jewish homeland in Palestine.

After World War I, the victorious Allied powers discussed the post-war settlement at Versailles in 1919, including the future status of the former provinces of the Turkish Empire. The San Remo Conference of 1920 under the auspices of the League of Nations awarded Britain the mandates of Iraq and Palestine; France was granted mandates over Syria and Lebanon. Generally the colonial powers sought to fix national borders in the Muslim world and the British in particular wished to establish stable monarchies. The year 1920 marked the low point of Islamic history as even the Turks fought to retain their grip upon their Anatolian heartlands. No great power now remained in the world to defend Muslim interests.

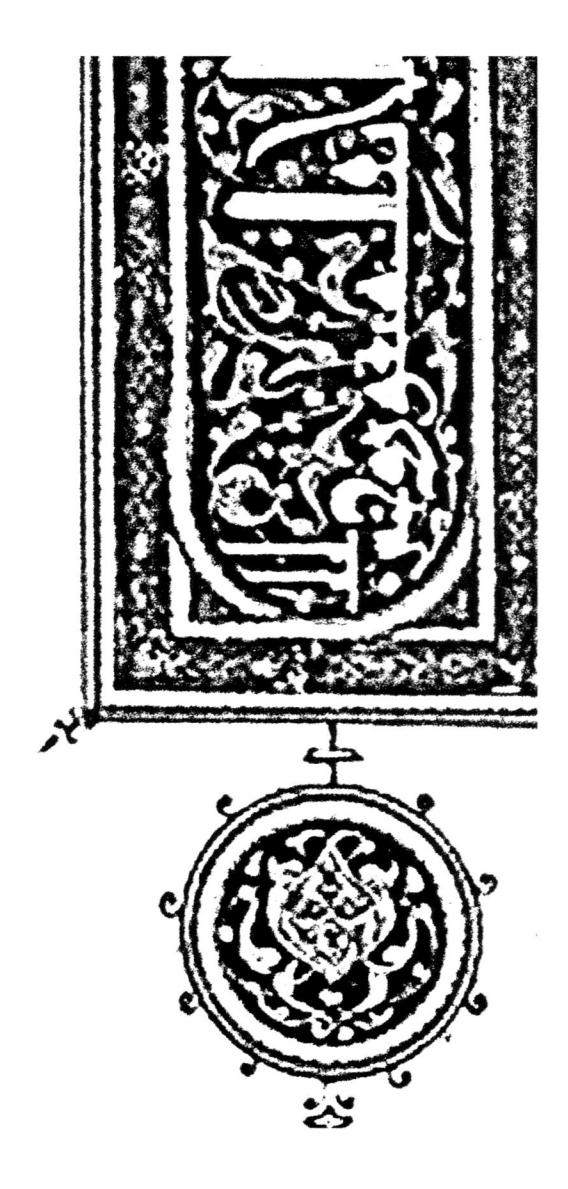

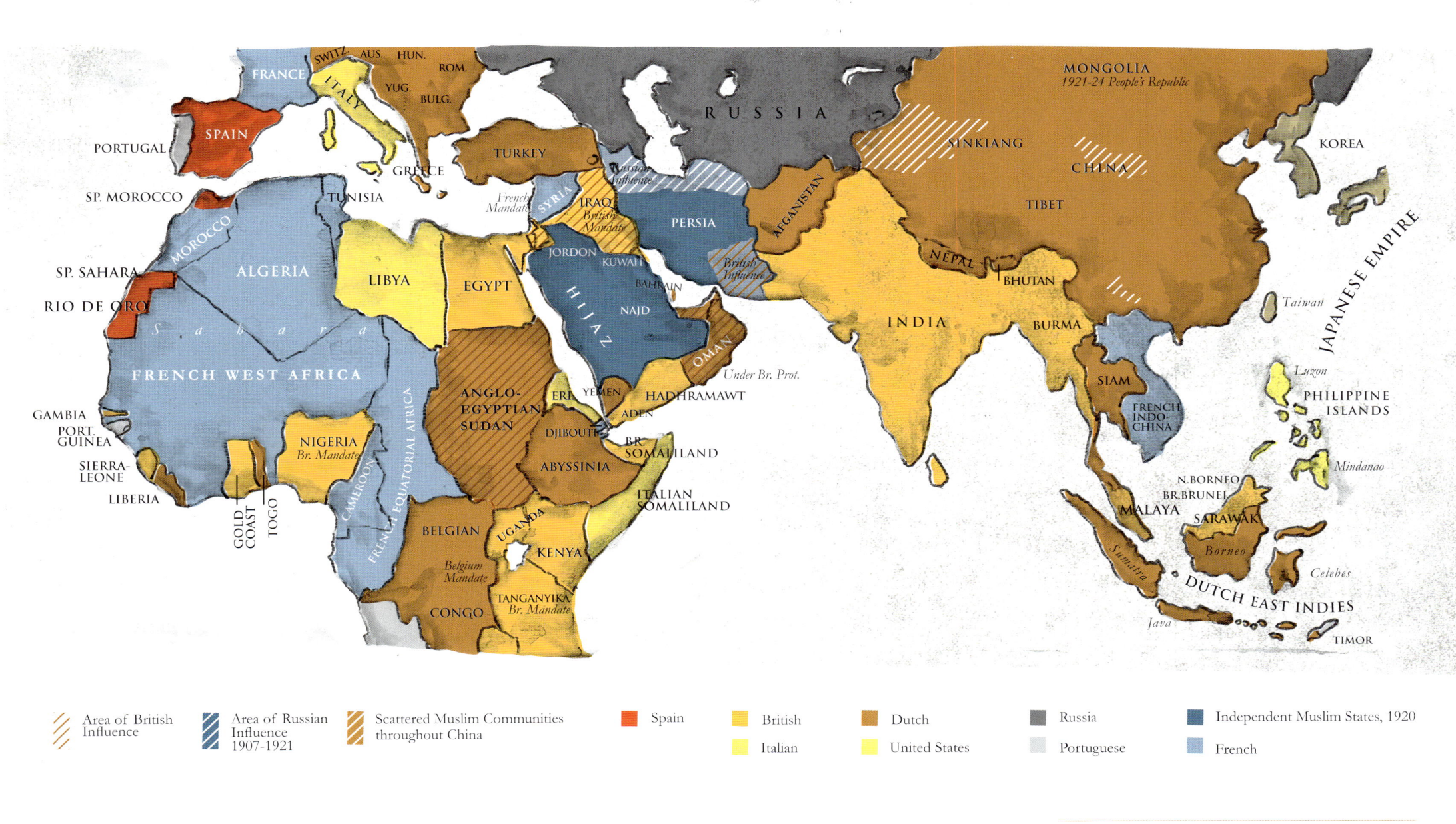

European Empires in the Muslim World, c.1920

Legend:
- Area of British Influence
- Area of Russian Influence 1907–1921
- Scattered Muslim Communities throughout China
- Spain
- British
- Dutch
- Russia
- Independent Muslim States, 1920
- Italian
- United States
- Portuguese
- French

THE RISE OF EUROPEAN POWER

1801CE 1216AH

Russian imperial advance into the Muslim world begins

1830CE 1246AH

The French colonial advance into Africa and the Middle East begins in Algeria

1857CE 1274AH

The Indian Revolt and the later establishment of the Raj, with India being ruled directly from London

The Muslim Response to European Colonialism

الرد عل الاستعمار

Under European colonialism, Muslims debated fiercely how to respond to the dramatic loss of power to determine the destiny of the *ummah*: were they to embrace the European way, or return to the fundamentals of their faith, or seek to achieve a synthesis of the two? Furthermore were they to achieve independence again through isolation, assimilation, adaption or resistance?

As the Muslim powers were no match for European colonisation, in the nineteenth century various resistance movements emerged, employing guerrilla tactics and often inspired by revivalist and Sufi teachings: Sayyid Ahmad Barelwi of India, 'Abd al-Qadir al-Jaza'iri of Algeria, Imam Shamil al-Daghastani of the Caucasus, 'Umar al-Mukhtar of Libya and Muhammad Ahmad, the self-declared Mahdi of Sudan. While none of these resistance movements could make a long-term military impact, the wider revivalist currents they represented among Sufis or the religious scholars did. The Tijaniyah, Qadiriyah, Sunusiyah, Idrisiyah and Sammaniyah orders in Africa, the reform movement of Ibn 'Abd al-Wahhab, the Naqshbandiyah order in the Middle East, the Caucasus, Central and South Asia and China, or the Fara'izi Movement of Bengal all laid greater emphasis on returning to the Prophet's example and rejecting the more speculative scholarly and mystical aspects of the Muslim heritage. Others focused on the need for religious reform and education like the Egyptian Salafiyah movement of Muhammad 'Abduh and the Deobandi and Aligarh movements of India. The pan-Islamist voice of Jamal al-Din al-Afghani (1838-1897) was a transitional figure who brought together the themes of Muslim unity, anti-colonial resistance and religious reform in a way that would be profoundly influential on revivalist movements of the twentieth century.

Jamal al-Din al-Afghani

1882–1922CE **1299–1340AH**
The British mandate in Egypt

Although Turkey survives, the British and the French divide up the Middle Eastern Ottoman territories

1916–1923CE **1335–1341 AH**

The Russo-Turkish War ends in Ottoman defeat

1877–1878CE **1294–1295AH**

c.1900CE **c.1318AH**
80% of Muslims live under European colonial rule

In the nineteenth century, modernising and nationalistic trends developed in the Muslim world that would come to fruition in the mid-twentieth century, not least by the Ottomans, who hoping to stave off their rapid decline, made Europeanising reforms. A similar endeavour was made by Muhammad 'Ali of Eygpt (r. 1805-1848) in reforming the military, the economy and education. His successor, Khedive Isma'il, with the help of the French, dug the strategically-important Suez canal which cut the distance between Europe and Asia for sea-borne commerce. Its opening in 1869 sparked an imperial rivalry between Britain and France to gain control over the canal; the British, in particular, did not wish to lose control of the main link between the motherland and its empire in Asia. After the failure of 'Urabi Pasha revolution, the British occupied Egypt in 1882 managing its economic affairs into the early twentieth century.

'Abd al-Qadir al-Jaza'iri

Muhammad 'Ali of Eygpt

THE RISE OF EUROPEAN POWER

The Modern Muslim Nation States

1342-1432 AH
1924-2011 CE

The last 100 years have been tumultuous ones for the Muslim world. While the period began with the height of Muslim subjugation under European rule, from the 1920s onwards modernised independent Muslim states began to emerge with the main period of decolonisation occurring through the 1940s to the 1970s. The later part of the twentieth century also saw a general Islamic revival while the end of the Cold War in the 1990s saw the emergence of greater hostility and conflict as the great Western powers saw this Islamic revival as a threat.

During the 1920s, despite the debilitating impact of the First World War on the European powers, the Muslim world retained a handful of independent Muslim states. In very different ways a handful of Muslim leaders were determined to modernise their countries and make them more independent of European power, as secular republicans like Kemal Ataturk of Turkey, as modernising kings like Reza Shah Pahlavi of Iran and King Amanullah of Afghanistan or as traditional leaders in alliance with religious scholars like the Zaydi Imam Yahya of northern Yemen and Ibn Sa'ud of Arabia. But collectively they could not provide leadership for a Muslim world that was under European colonial rule.

Mustafa Kemal Ataturk's abolition of the caliphate in 1924 was met with incomprehension and consternation. Attempts to revive the office were dashed by the emerging strength of Muslim nationalism and the rivalry of various claimants, despite huge mass movements in support of its revival in India and Indonesia. After the Europeans, weakened by the Second World War, dismantled their empires, the main political response to independence was nationalist and secular in spirit and showed the extent of European influence, which had created legal systems that did not recognise the *Shari'ah* and schools that did not teach Islamic knowledge.

The Last Caliph, Abdulmecid II

Deposed from the throne by the Ankara Assembly, Colour lithograph from "Le Petit Journal", 1924

Mustafa Kemal Ataturk

The founding father of the modern secular republic of Turkey in the 1920s

THE MODERN MUSLIM NATION STATES

A generation came to power in the Muslim world that was secular in taste and outlook; by and large, the religious scholars and the Sufi orders were marginalised as representing the past. *Shari'ah* courts were abolished and many of the religious endowments (*awqaf*) and the religious institutions they supported were put under state control. For many devout Muslims, independence merely represented an exchange of secular elites, but even so the very fact of freedom from alien rule brought a new-found confidence and hope.

Most Muslim peoples gained their independence between the 1940s and the early 1970s, although some Muslim states like Egypt and Iraq had achieved a limited independence before the Second World War. A quarter remained under non-Muslim rule in China, India and the Soviet Union, the latter having to wait for independence until the fall of the Soviet Empire in 1991. The violent fallout to the ending of communist influence in the Balkans meant that Muslim-majority states like Bosnia (1995) and Kosovo (2008) only emerged with a degree of international support and protection. Some freedom struggles attained independence through negotiation while others were achieved through great sacrifice – after 130 years of French rule, the eight years of the Algerian War of Independence cost up to a million lives. If many states became secular and nationalist in outlook, others sought to become modern Islamic states like Saudi Arabia (1932) and Pakistan (1947), from which its eastern wing, Bangladesh, became independent after civil war in 1971.

Reza Shah Pahlavi of Iran

The modernising king posing in military uniform (1925)

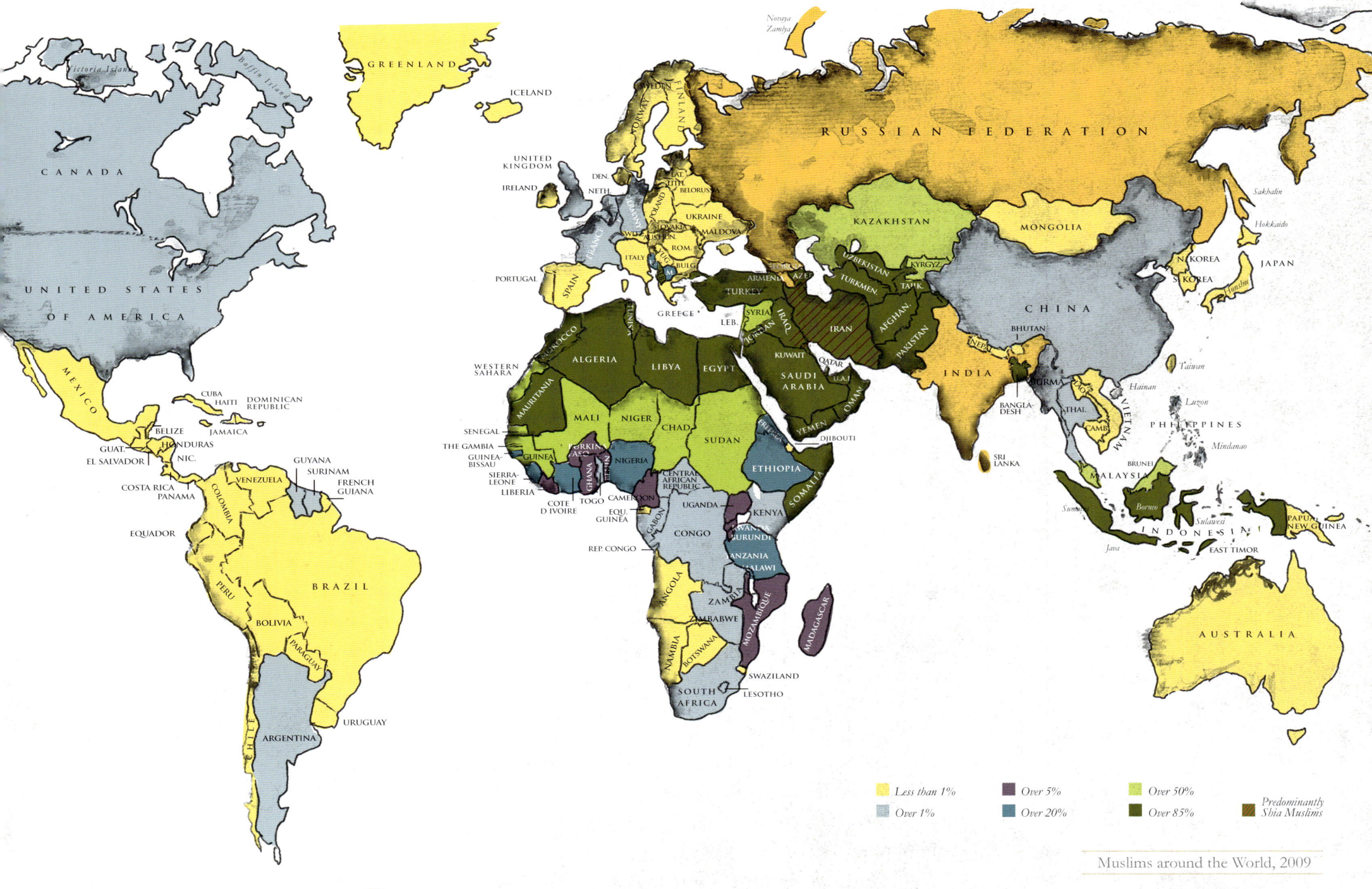

THE MODERN MUSLIM NATION STATES

Muslims around the World, 2009

Legend:
- Less than 1%
- Over 1%
- Over 5%
- Over 20%
- Over 50%
- Over 85%
- Predominantly Shia Muslims

1917 CE 1335AH

Britain pledges to establish a national Jewish homeland in Palestine

1932CE 1351AH

Iraq gains independence from the British

The Second World War; Hitler orders the Holocaust against the Jews

1939–1945CE 1358–1364AH

However it was quickly seen that in many ways the Muslim world remained dependent not only on Europe, but increasingly upon the new nuclear superpowers, the United States and the Soviet Union, that faced each other during the Cold War (1945-1991). Their military bases remained scattered through the Muslim world and Western businesses kept tight control over the most developed and profitable parts of their economies, notably oil, which had been discovered in abundance in the Middle East. Mossadeq of Iran (1951-1953) unsuccessfully tried to nationalise the Anglo-Iranian Oil Company before he was overthrown by Western-backed coup. More successful was Nasser of Egypt (1952-1970) who nationalised the Suez Canal, successfully resisting Israeli, French and British military retaliation. Attempting to do more than just play off the superpowers, some Muslim nations supported the non-aligned Bandung movement of 1955, experimented with Arab federalism (the short-lived United Arab Republic

Nasser of Egypt

Held aloft by a jubilant crowd after reclaiming the Suez Canal in 1956

The Arab-Israel War of 1967

Up to 20,000 refugees flee across the shattered Allenby Bridge into Jordan

1948CE 1367AH
Establishment of Israel, known to Palestinians as the 'year of catastrophe'

The Suez Crisis; Egypt nationalises the Suez Canal
1956CE 1375AH

Lebanon, Syria, Jordan and Pakistan become independent

1946–1947CE 1365–1367AH

1954–1962CE 1374–1382AH
The Algerian war of independence from French rule

of Egypt and Syria, 1958-1961), and formed an economic alliance to control oil production, the Organisation of Petroleum Exporting Countries (OPEC) in 1960.

What symbolised most sharply continuing Muslim weakness was the establishment of Israel on the Arab land of Palestine in 1948 with the support of Britain. In the Arab-Israeli wars of 1948, 1956, 1967 and 1973, the Arabs had been defeated and much new land was occupied – all of Palestine, Egypt's Sinai Peninsula and Syria's Golan Heights. The Palestinian people were left stateless on a tiny fraction of their former land in the Gaza Strip and the West Bank. Zionism was unsurprisingly seen as yet another chapter in European colonialism, again supported by the West, and by the United States in particular, especially after the 1967 war.

Mossadeq of Iran

A popular Iranian leader who was overthrown in an American-backed coup in 1953

THE MODERN MUSLIM NATION STATES

◆ A MUSLIM COMMUNITY IN BEIJING

Today the ancient civilisation of China is linked with increasing economic power and cultural influence, but not so often with Islam. It is thought that China will be the world's largest economy sometime after 2020, and the Olympics of 2008 put the country and its capital under an international spotlight. Yet if travellers were to head towards the traditional alleys (*hutong*) in Beijing's southern quarters that are rapidly giving way to highways and skyscrapers, they would come across an ancient mosque, the Niujie ('Oxen Street'), that celebrated its thousandth anniversary in 1997. Some 12,000 Muslims live around the mosque, with up to 200,000 in Beijing as a whole.

Like many other Beijing neighbourhoods, there is an entrance arch, but it is in the details that its Muslim character can be identified: the inscriptions on the arch are in both Mandarin and Arabic. Niujie District has housed an important *halal* beef market for 400 years, and pork, the preferred meat in the rest of the city, is absent here. The locals dress in a distinctive Muslim fashion. The older men still wear the traditional fur caps and long fur-lined jackets, with their trousers tucked into their boots; some of the younger women wear headscarves.

One could walk right past the Niujie without realising that it was a mosque, unless one knew what to look for. The mosque has the traditional Chinese architectural features of curling roofs and glazed tiles, along with its squat and square minaret. At the entrance, there are two signs in Mandarin: one has the term for a mosque, 'Temple of the Pure and True Doctrine'; the other reads 'the good path to heaven'. Inside, the walls are carved and painted with a six-hundred-year-old *mihrab*, while, outside in the courtyard, there are carefully-tended bonsai trees in the courtyard, along with a large bronze pot, inscribed with Chinese characters, which is used to prepare regular meals for the poor. This is an ancient Muslim community that learnt during the years of communist Mao Zedong's Cultural Revolution (1966-1971) to hold onto its faith unobtrusively and quietly in a period when many mosques were shut down or even destroyed. After Chairman Mao's death, restrictions on religious practice were gradually lifted, and millennial celebrations for the mosque in 1997 were officially supported.

The ancient Niujie mosque, Beijing

THE MODERN MUSLIM NATION STATES

1967 CE 1387 AH

The Six Day War between Israel and her Arab neighbours

1979 CE 1399 AH

Ayatollah Khomeini proclaims the Islamic Republic of Iran;

1979–1989 CE 1399–1410 AH

The Soviet occupation of Afghanistan

All this discontent at Muslim weakness – and fact that the secular Muslim republics and monarchies were all too often authoritarian in nature – led towards a general Islamic revival in the second half of the twentieth century. The anti-colonial and reformist Islamic movements of the eighteenth and nineteenth centuries were further built upon by movements that emerged between 1920 and 1950, seeking, with the end of the caliphate, a means by which to create more Islamic societies and governments like the Tablighi Jama'at of India (1926), the Muslim Brotherhood of Egypt (1928) and the Jama'at-i Islami of India (1941), all of which became international movements after the Second World War.

After independence, as traditional Muslims, who were moving into the rapidly-expanding cities, sought to reassert their values, a competition emerged for their support between governments, even the more secular ones like Turkey, and the Islamic movements; this competition intensified after the Arab defeat by Israel in 1967. Notably in the 1960s and 1970s, the establishment of the missionary Muslim World League in 1962, the Organisation of the Islamic Conference, the Muslim version of the United Nations, in 1969, and the International Islamic Development Bank in 1973 reflected this surge in pan-Islamic sentiment. This resurgence even found an echo amongst new Muslim communities in the West with figures like Malcolm X (1925-1965) (*see page 128*). The OPEC boycott of Western nations supporting Israel after the 1973 Arab-Israeli war, causing a global price shock, indicated a growing political confidence. Yet at the same time, radical splinters, impatient with the slow pace of change, broke away from the mainstream Islamic revivalists, notably a militant faction around Saudi Muhammad al-'Utaybi, proclaimed as the Mahdi in Makkah in 1979, and Excommunication and Flight (Takfir wa'l-Hijrah) that assassinated President Sadat of Egypt in 1981.

The break-up of the Soviet Union

Azerbaijanis march for freedom in 1991

1990–1991 CE 1411–1412 AH
The First Gulf War

1991 CE 1412 AH

The collapse of the Soviet Union; the Central Asian Muslim states become independent

The Iran-Iraq War
1980–1988 CE 1400–1409 AH

Ayatollah Khomeini

On his return to Iran in 1979, prior to the birth of the Islamic Republic

The pivotal year of 1979 marked a decisive turning point. After the overthrow of the Shah of Iran, the Iranian Revolution allowed Ayatollah Ruhollah Khomeini (1902-1989) to establish an Islamic Republic, providing the first full Islamic alternative to the model of secular nationalism that Ataturk had inspired in the 1920s. None of the other attempts at Islamising state and society before or after – Zia-ul-Haq's Pakistan, Muammar Gaddafi's Libya with his eclectic Islamic socialism, Numairi's Sudan, the Taliban's Afghanistan – had so much impact. Yet at the same time, the Shi'i specificity of Khomeini's doctrine of the rule of the jurist (*vilayat-i faqih*) could find no easy equivalent in Sunni Islam, with the partial exception of the Taliban, who, as 'students' of religious law, sought to interpret and apply *Shari'ah* in Afghanistan. The years since 1979 have proved difficult for the Muslim world as conflict and war have become more widespread. During the Cold War, the Muslim nations attempted to balance the competing superpowers to their best interest. But, with the collapse of the Soviet Union in 1991, America and her allies were able to extend their military and political power in the Muslim world in the first Gulf War (1990-1991) or more commonly by supporting authoritarian regimes against political Islamic revival, for example in Algeria and Egypt. Internally, ethnic and religious tensions have flared up into civil war in the Muslim world in Somalia, Sudan, the Lebanon, Afghanistan and Algeria. The Palestinians have not achieved freedom and independence from Israel, despite two major uprisings (1987-1993, 2000-2005). Saddam Hussain of Iraq (1979-2003) invaded both Iran (1980-1988) and Kuwait (1990-1991).

THE MODERN MUSLIM NATION STATES

Al-Qa'ida attacks on Washington and New York, the US-led invasion of Afghanistan

2001CE 1422AH

The last great Cold War conflict was the Soviet occupation of Afghanistan (1979-1989). Out of this conflict grew a mobile international jihad movement that went on to fight in Bosnia, Kosovo, Chechnya and Kashmir, wherever Muslim minorities were under attack by non-Muslims. From 1998, a faction under Osama bin Laden, al-Qa'ida, decided to target Western countries directly – mostly infamously with the terrorist attacks on New York and Washington DC in 2001. This resulted in the American-led invasions of Afghanistan (2001) and Iraq (2003) as well as proxy wars in the Lebanon (2006) and Somalia (2007) all conducted in the name of a 'war on terror'. Yet al-Qa'ida, with minimal support in the Muslim world, has been able to inspire a tiny fringe to attack civilians indiscriminately in the West and in the Muslim world, feeding on a larger sense of political powerlessness that exists among Muslims today.

Yet despite the crushing of the Green Revolution in Iran in 2009, young Muslims using the internet to mobilise themselves have succeeded in forcing democratic change in Tunisia, Egypt and Libya in 2011, which will have a major political impact upon the greater Middle East and the whole Muslim world.

The journey through Islamic history is not yet complete. The future is uncertain yet it appears humanity is now obliged to find common solutions to challenges like poverty, environmental degradation, global warming and political conflict and instability. Despite these heavy challenges, Muslims can still work to harmonise contemporary life and Islamic traditions to spark once again the historic genius of their civilisation to achieve new heights of greatness in the future.

The Iraq War of 2003

More than a million people march in London against the war

A JOURNEY THROUGH ISLAMIC HISTORY

2003CE 1424AH
The US-led invasion of Iraq

2011CE 1432AH
Overthrow of the Tunisian, Egyptian and Libyan regimes

The Egyptian Revolution of 2011

Egyptians celebrate the ousting of President Mubarak in Tahrir Square in Cairo

Palestinian and Jewish Land 1945

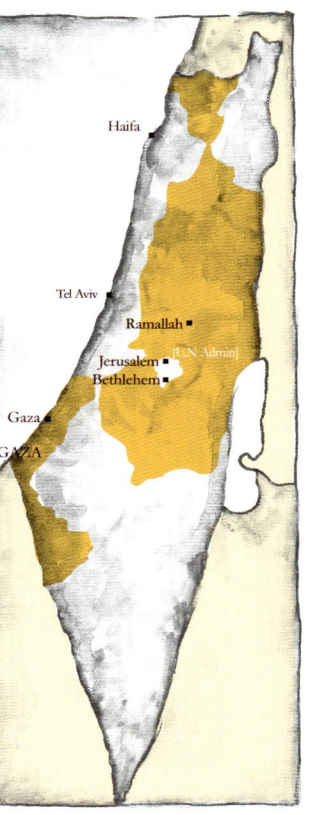

UN Partition Plan, 1947

Palestinian and Jewish Land 1948-1967

Palestinian and Jewish Land 1999

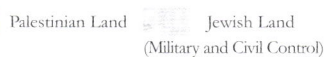

Palestinian Land   Jewish Land (Military and Civil Control)

THE MODERN MUSLIM NATION STATES

MALCOLM X
AMERICA'S CHAMPION OF ISLAM

Malcolm X (1925-1965), along with Martin Luther King, Jr., were the two great figures of the African American civil rights movement of the second half of the twentieth century. The older stereotype would have King as the Christian minister who preached non-violence and inter-racial harmony, with Malcolm cast as the radical Muslim leader who promoted violent confrontation and racial hatred, and who wanted to overthrow the system 'by any means necessary'. Yet the view that predominates in America today tends to emphasise their similarities: both worked to strengthen black communities and their institutions, condemned black-on-black violence and drugs, opposed the Vietnam War and worked for the cause of global human rights.

Born Malcolm Little in Omaha, Nebraska, the son of a Baptist minister, the family experienced racial violence and harassment; his father was brutally murdered and his mother, caring for seven children, suffered a breakdown and was institutionalised. Malcolm fell into a life of crime as a young man, becoming a pimp, hustler and drug dealer, and was known on the street as 'Detroit Little'. Sentenced to 10 years of hard labour in prison, Malcolm reassessed his life and turned to religion, joining the Nation of Islam movement, headed by Elijah Muhammad, a heterodox group which believed that all white people were devils created by black scientists, but which also championed the rights of the poor and disadvantaged black people in the inner cities. On his release Malcolm Little was given the name Malcolm X and, with his intelligence, eloquence and charisma, he built up the Nation of Islam into a national movement with over 100,000 members. By 1954, he had become the Nation's official spokesman. To the political establishment, his outspoken attack on racial injustice had him dubbed as 'the angriest black man in America', but his call for black liberation, economic self-help and political empowerment was in fact crucial to the development of the civil rights movement. Yet, by 1964, Malcolm had outgrown the Nation which he found to be too apolitical and left to form his own organisations, the Muslim Mosque Inc., and its political wing, the Organization of Afro-American Unity. In the same year, he performed the Hajj for the first time which was a life-transforming event.

He embraced Sunni Islam, and became El-Hajj Malik El-Shabbaz. He rejected the racial doctrines of the Nation, accepting Islam's message of the equality and brotherhood of all humanity, where he met 'blonde-haired, blue-eyed men I could call my brothers'. He returned to the United States with a new message of racial and cultural tolerance in America itself, as well as championing international human rights causes – for justice and freedom for the world's poor and downtrodden. However in February 1965, just short of his fortieth birthday, Malcolm was brutally assassinated before he had a chance to develop his ideas further and take them to the world as he had by then become an international figure.

What was lost that terrible night in 1965 was the one great figure who had the potential to unite the radicals and moderates in the civil rights movement, American black activists with Asian, African and Caribbean nations, and who could have created bridges of understanding between the Muslim world and the West. Yet despite his premature death, Malcolm's legacy is an ever-growing one – and he has inspired subsequent generations to fight for racial justice and equality not only in America but around the world.

Malcolm X (1925-1965)

THE MODERN MUSLIM NATION STATES

SHORT GLOSSARY

معاه الكلمات

AH:
After Hijrah – the period after the migration of the Prophet from Makkah to Madinah on 16th July 622 CE, which marks the start of the Hijri Calendar.

AHL AL-KITAB:
literally the People of the Book or non-Muslim subjects of religions that possess a scripture; this Qur'anic term usually applies to Jews and Christians.

AL-AMIN:
literally, the honest; the trustworthy; a title of respect given to Prophet Muhammad (peace be upon him).

BAY'AH:
literally an oath of allegiance to an authority; oath of loyalty.

BANU ISRA'IL:
Israelites; Banu is prefixed to the name of the founder of a family house, to a tribe or to a people.

BH:
Before Hijrah – the period before the migration (Hijrah) of the Prophet from Makkah to Madinah on 16th July 622 CE, which marks the start of the Hijri Calendar.

CE:
Common Era – marks the start of the Christian calendar at the birth of Jesus.

HADITH (PL. AHADITH):
comprises of statements of the Prophet regarding religious duties, his advice and admonition, his own actions, and his reactions to the words or deeds of others in his presence.

HAJJ:
Pilgrimage; Rituals of Islamic pilgrimage performed at Makkah and 'Arafah.

IBN:
son; (plural Abna' or Banu); for instance, Banu Hashim or Hashimites.

'ID AL-ADHA:
Festival of Sacrifice after the Pilgrimage; a festival initiated by Abraham (peace be upon him).

'ID AL-FITR:
Festival of Zakat al-Fitr at the end of Ramadan, the month of fasting.

ISRA':
lit. journey; the Prophet's night journey from Makkah to Jerusalem in the company of the archangel Gabriel (Jibril, 'alayhi as-salam).

JIHAD:
an all-out effort to implement Islam; an exertion; fighting/struggle for the cause of Islam.

JIZYAH:
poll-tax; a fixed tax on every adult able-bodied non-Muslim subject living within the territory of an Islamic state or empire (priests, the disabled and the sick, and women and children were exempted from paying it) Jizyah ranged from one to three dinars per annum.

KHALIFAH:
(Ar.), literally successor, deputy, representative, caliph; a successor to the Prophet as head of the Islamic state.

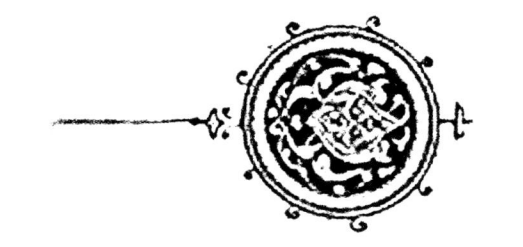

SHORT GLOSSARY

Khilafah:
literally the office of the Khalifah or Caliph; deputyship, vicegerency.

Mi'raj:
literally ascension; the ascension of the Prophet Muhammad (pbuh) to Heaven in the company of the archangel Gabriel.

Mu'tazilah:
a theological school of thought that flourished between the eighth and tenth centuries CE in Basrah and Baghdad, which focused on the centrality of human reason in interpreting religion.

Qarmatians:
A small Shia Isma'ili sect of Eastern Arabia that flourished in the ninth century CE, best known for their revolt against the 'Abbasids, and their sacking of Makkah.

Qira'ah:
literally, recitation; the recitation of the Qur'an.

al-Qur'an:
literally 'reading or recitation'; the sacred scripture of Islam, referring to the collection of revelations received by the Prophet from God.

Quraysh:
The dominant tribe of Makkah to which the Prophet belonged, which initially opposed the religion of Islam before reconciling to it.

Transoxiana:
This is the ancient term used for the part of Central Asia between the Amu Darya and Syr Darya rivers, which today comprises of Uzbekistan, Tajikistan and southwest Kazakhstan.

Zakah or Zakat:
(literally purification); an obligatory financial contribution by a Muslim for the welfare of the poor and the needy.

INDEX

'Abbas I, 96-8
'Abbasids, 36-69, 81, 83; of Cairo, 75, 88
'Abdallah al-Ma'mun, 40, 43
'Abd al-Malik ibn Marwan, 28, 32, 35
'Abd al-Rahman al-Nasir li-Din Allah, 46-7
'Abd al-Rahman ibn Mu'awiyah al-Dakhil, 46
'Abd al-Qadir al-Jaza'iri, 112
'Abdalwadids, 77
Abdulhamid II, 69, 95
Abu Bakr, 3, 17-21, 24-5, 69
Abu Hanifah, 41
Abu Ja'far al-Mansur, 38, 46
Abu'l-'Abbas al-Saffah, 38, 46
Aceh, 109
'Adud al-Dawlah, 57
Afghanistan, 51, 58-9, 96, 110, 116, 125-6
Afsharids, 97
Aghlabids, 38, 45, 50, 54
Ahmad ibn Asad, 51
Ahmad ibn Hanbal, 40-1
Ahmad ibn Tulun, 53
Akbar, 98, 100, 103-4
Albania, 84, 92
Algebra, 40
Algeria, 50, 54, 78, 88, 109, 112, 118, 125
'Ali ibn Abi Talib, 17, 19, 23
Aligarh, 112
Almohads, 45-6, 49, 77
Almoravids, 45-6, 49
Alp Arslan, 62, 64
Anatolia, 64, 68, 76, 84, 95, 110
Arabia, 4, 9-12, 17-8, 53, 62, 110
Arabic, 24, 30, 40-2, 47-8, 72, 75, 122
Arabs, 10, 24, 34, 37, 47, 49, 121

Architecture, 30, 47, 49, 55, 86-7, 93, 98, 104-5, 122
Aquinas, 48
'Asabiyah (Solidarity), 10, 78-9
Ascension (Mi'raj) of the Prophet, 5
Astronomy, 40, 62
Awqaf (Religious Endowments), 118
Awrangzeb, 101
Ayatollah Khomeini, 125
'Ayn Jalut, 68, 72, 76, 81
Ayyubids, 45, 63-4, 66, 68, 71-2
Azerbaijan, 96, 109
Al-Azhar, 55

Babur, 100
Baghdad, 38, 40-3, 45, 52, 57, 59, 62, 68, 75, 81, 96
Balfour Declaration, 110
Balkans, 84, 90-2, 110, 118
Bangladesh, 118
Basrah, 17, 22, 25, 32
Battles, 4, 18, 20, 23-4, 30, 62, 64, 66, 72, 84, 100-1
Baybars I al-Bunduqdari, 68, 75, 81
Beijing, 122
Beirut, 72
Belles-Lettres (Adab), 41
Bengal, 83, 100-1, 112
Berbers, 27-8, 37, 46-7, 49-50, 54, 77
Al-Biruni, 40, 58
Black Stone (Hajar al-Aswad), 53
Bosnia, 92, 118, 126
Britain, 95, 101, 107-11, 113, 120
Bukhara, 34, 60, 109
Al-Bukhari, 40
Bulgaria, 84, 110
Buwayhids/Buyids, 41, 44-5, 57, 59, 62
Byzantines, 2, 18, 27, 32-3, 38, 42, 50, 62, 64, 87-8

Cairo, 53, 55, 67-8, 75, 78, 81
Calendars, 8, 22, 62
Caliphate (Khilafah), 16-25, 28, 37-8, 40, 44-6, 54, 57, 62, 68-9, 75, 81, 88, 95, 116, 124
Calligraphy, 55, 91
Caravanserais, 86, 90
Caucasus, 30, 72, 91, 112
Central Asia, 30, 34, 58, 62, 68, 76, 96, 100, 107-8
Ceramics, 93, 98
Charles Martel, 30
Chechnya, 72, 126
China, 34, 37, 112, 118, 122
Christians, 3, 10, 32, 46-9, 55, 64-5, 86, 90, 92, 110, 128
Communism, 118, 122
Constantinople, 2-3, 27, 68, 88, 110
Conversion, 2-3, 5, 47, 68, 76, 90, 92
Convivencia, 48-9
Cordoba, 28, 46, 48-9
Crusades, 49, 55, 63-8, 71-2, 81
Cyprus, 27, 72

Damascus, 28, 30, 32-3, 56, 67, 72, 78, 81
Devshirme (Military Conscription), 86, 90-2
Delhi, 100-1
Deobandis, 112
Dhimmis (Protected Peoples), 48, 92
Dome of the Rock, 30, 63, 72
Dutch, 107, 109

East India Company, 101, 109
Education, 33, 55, 62, 67, 91, 95, 112-3
Egypt, 3, 18, 22, 30, 46, 53, 55-6, 63-4, 66, 68, 71-2, 74-5, 78, 81, 88, 107-8, 113, 118, 121, 124, 124-7
Elijah Muhammad, 128

Europe, 30, 37, 48-50, 64, 66, 69, 84, 92, 95, 97-8, 101, 107-13, 116, 120

Al-Farabi, 40
Fara'izis, 112
Fatimids, 45-6, 50, 54-6, 63
Al-Firdawsi, 58, 60-1
First World War, 95, 116
Fiqh (Jurisprudence), 41
France, 30, 48, 64, 71, 95, 107-10, 113, 118, 120

Genghis (Chenghiz) Khan, 68, 100
Geometry, 40
Al-Ghazali, 41, 62
Ghaznavids, 45, 50, 59, 62
Granada, 46, 78

Hafsids, 77
Harun al-Rashid, 38, 42-3, 50
Hayrettin Barbarosa, 92
Hijaz, 10, 55, 88
Historians, 41, 68, 78-9, 105
Hospitals, 43, 57, 86
House of Wisdom (Bayt al-Hikmah), 40, 42
Hulagu Khan, 68
Humayun, 100
Hungary, 84, 92
Husayn ibn 'Ali, 28

Ibn 'Abd al-Wahhab, 112
Ibn Haytham, 40, 55
Ibn Hazm, 47
Ibn Khaldun, 74, 78-9
Ibn Rushd, 47, 49
Ibn Sa'ud, 116
Ibn Sina, 41, 47
Ibn Tufayl, 47
Idrisids, 45-6
Ifriqiyah, 27, 46, 50, 54
Ikhshidids, 45, 56
Ilkhanids, 64, 66
India, 58-9, 76, 83, 100-3, 108, 112, 116, 118, 124

Indochina, 107
International Islamic Development Bank, 124
Iran, 61, 68, 76, 81, 83, 97, 116, 120, 125-6
Iranian Revolution, 125-6
Iraq, 10, 21-2, 30, 45, 53-4, 57, 62, 66, 68, 110, 118, 125-6
Isfahan, 96, 98
Islam, 6-7
Isma'il I, 96-7
Isma'ilis, 53-6, 66
Israel, 120-1, 124-5
Istanbul, 88, 93, 98
Italy, 50, 55
Iznik, 87, 93

Jahangir, 100
Al-Jahiz, 41
Jalal al-Din al-Suyuti, 74
Jama'at-i Islami, 124
Jamal al-Din al-Afghani, 112
Janissaries, 90-2
Jerusalem, 8, 20, 30, 63-4, 66-7, 72
Jews, 10, 47-9, 55, 63, 90, 110
Jihad, 126

Kabul, 52, 100
Kashmir, 100, 126
Kemal Ataturk, 69, 116, 125
Khadijah bint Khuwaylid, 5, 14-15
Khawarij, 23, 34, 50
Al-Khawarizmi, 40, 47
Khurasan, 38, 45, 51-2, 62
Khusraw Parviz, 2
Khutbah (Friday sermon), 8, 46, 57, 62, 69
Kosovo, 92, 118, 126
Kufah, 17, 22, 25, 32, 54
Kurds, 63, 66, 96

Lahore, 103
Law, 2, 12, 37, 67, 92, 126
Lebanon, 110, 125
Libraries, 33, 42, 47, 55, 68, 102

Libya, 71, 112, 125-6
Literature, 41, 47-9, 57, 60-1

Macedonia, 84, 110
Madinah, 2, 5, 8, 20, 22, 25, 32, 35, 72
Madrasah (Seminary), 41, 62, 86, 98
Mahmud ibn Sebuktigin, 58-60, 76
Maimonides, 49
Makkah, 1-2, 4-5, 8-10, 14, 20, 22, 25, 53, 72, 124
Malcolm X, 124, 128-9
Malik ibn Anas, 41
Malta, 50, 92
Al-Maqrizi, 74, 78
Marinids, 77
Mamluks, 64, 68, 70-81, 88
Mao Zedong, 122
Mathematics, 40
Mawalis, 28, 34, 35
Medicine, 40, 43, 48
Mehmed II the Conqueror, 88
Merv, 96
Mihna (Inquiry), 40
Mihrab (Prayer Niche), 32, 122
Minbar (Pulpit), 32
Moldova, 92
Mongols, 45, 64, 68, 71-2, 76, 81
Morocco, 45-6, 83, 110
Mosques, 8, 22, 25, 30, 32-3, 49, 53, 55, 69, 72, 86-7, 93, 98, 122
Mossadeq, 120
Mu'awiyah ibn Abi Sufyan, 27-8
Al-Mu'izz li-Din Allah, 55
Mughals, 83, 85, 100-5
Muhammad 'Abduh, 112
Muhammad Ahmad, 112
Muhammad Ali, 113
Muhammad al-Shafi'i, 41
Muhammad ibn al-Qasim al-Thaqafi, 34
Muhammad ibn Tughj, 56
Mu'in al-Din Chishti, 104
Mumtaz Mahal, 103-4
Muslim Brotherhood, 124

Muslim ibn Hajjaj, 40
Muslim World League, 124
Muzaffar Sayf al-Din Qutuz, 72, 81

Al-Najashi, 2
Napoleon, 107
Nasrids, 46, 77
Nasser, 120
Nation of Islam, 128
Nishapur, 45, 52, 62
Nizam al-Mulk, 41, 62
Normans, 50
North Africa, 27-8, 30, 34, 46, 50, 55, 77-8, 81
Nur al-Din Zangi, 55, 63

Oil, 120-1
Oman, 2, 53, 55
OPEC, 121, 124
Ophthalmology, 55
Optics, 40, 55
Organisation of the Islamic Conference, 124
Osama bin Laden, 126
Osman I, 84
Ottomans, 68-9, 75, 78, 83-96, 108, 110, 113

Pakistan, 118, 125
Palestine, 18, 55, 68, 72, 110, 121, 125
People of the Book (Ahl al-Kitab), 48
Persia, 2-3, 18, 22, 30, 45, 52, 54, 57-62, 68, 75-6, 96-8, 110
Persian, 61
Philosophy (Falsafah), 40-2, 49
Pilgrimage (Hajj), 4-5, 7-9, 12, 20, 43, 53, 104, 129
Piri Reis, 92
Poetry, 10, 24, 38, 47-8, 52, 60, 62, 93
Poll-Tax (Jizyah), 35
Pope Urban II, 64
Prayer (Salah), 8, 24, 32
Prophet Muhammad, 1-15, 17, 20, 22, 24
Prophetic Tradition (Hadith), 40

al-Qa'ida, 126

Qajars, 97
Qarakhanids, 62
Qarmatians, 45, 53
Qazwin, 96
Qayrawan, 27, 54
Qiblah (Direction of Prayer), 8, 32
Qur'an, 2-4, 12, 22, 24-5, 40
Quraysh, 8-9, 20, 25

Ramadan, 5, 7-8
Reconquista, 47, 49
Reza Shah Pahlavi, 116
Richard I, 67
Russia, 69, 72, 95, 107, 109

Safavids, 83, 85, 96-9
Saffarids, 38, 45, 52
Salah al-Din al-Ayyubi, 55, 63-4, 66-7
Saljuqs, 41, 45, 57, 59, 62-4
Samanids, 38, 45, 51-2, 59-60, 62
Samarqand, 34
San Remo Conference, 110
Sasanians, 2-10, 18, 57
Saudi Arabia, 118
Sayyid Ahmad Barelwi, 112
Science, 40-2, 47-8, 55, 57-8, 62, 93, 107
Second World War, 116, 118, 124
Selim I, 68, 86, 88, 90, 96
Seville, 28, 46
Shah Jahan, 100, 103-5
Shamil al-Daghastani, 112
Shi'ah, 37, 116, 118, 125
Shi'ahs, 23, 34, 41, 45, 53, 54, 57, 69, 96-7, 125
Sicily, 50, 55
Sinan, 86-7, 91, 93
Sind, 34, 55, 100
Soviet Union, 118, 120, 125-6
Spain (Al-Andalus), 28, 30, 34, 45-9
Sudan, 108, 112, 125
Suez Canal, 108, 113, 120
Sufism, 96, 112, 118

Suleyman the Magnificent, 86, 92, 98
Sunnah (Prophet's Example), 12, 22
Sunnis, 23, 51, 59, 62, 66, 69, 72, 81, 96, 100, 129
Sykes-Picot Agreement, 110
Syria, 18, 21-2, 27, 30, 35, 46, 53, 55-6, 62-4, 66, 68, 71, 73, 81, 88, 107, 110, 121

Al-Tabari, 41
Tablighi Jama'at, 124
Tabriz, 68, 96
Tahirids, 38, 45, 52
Taj Mahal, 103-5
Tamerlane (Timur), 78-9, 84, 100
Tariq ibn Ziyad, 28
Taxes, 35, 79, 100-1
Textiles, 93, 98
Theology, 23, 40-1, 47-9
Thousand and One Nights, 38, 43
Trade, 10, 14, 42, 47, 74, 101, 113, 121
Transoxiana, 34, 38, 45, 51-2, 60
Tughril Beg, 62
Tulunids, 45, 53
Tunisia, 27, 38, 50, 54, 109, 126
Turks, 37, 59, 62, 68, 72, 84, 86, 90-1, 95, 100, 110, 116, 124

'Ubaydullah al-Mahdi, 54
Ulema (scholars of the religious sciences), 40, 92, 100, 112, 116, 118
'Umar al-Mukhtar, 112
'Umar ibn 'Abd al-'Aziz, 28-9, 35-6
'Umar ibn al-Khattab, 17-19, 21, 24-5, 27, 64
'Umar Khayyam, 62
Umayyads, 19, 23, 26-35, 69; of Spain, 45-6, 48-9
Ummah (community), 2, 69, 110, 112
United States of America, 120, 126, 128-9
'Uthman ibn al-'Affan, 17, 19, 25
Urdu, 102

Victoria, 101
Vienna, 92, 95

Walid ibn 'Abd al-Malik, 28, 32-3, 35
Wars, 10; Aceh, 108; Algerian, 118; civil, 23, 46, 118; Cold, 115, 120, 125-6; First Gulf, 125; First World, 110; Israeli, 121; on terror, 126; Second World, 116, 118, 124; tribal, 10; Vietnam, 128

Ya'qub ibn al-Layth al-Saffar, 52
Yazid ibn Mu'awiyah, 28
Yemen, 2, 10, 42, 55, 78, 92, 116

Zakah, 9, 21
Zands, 97
Zionism, 121
Zoroastrians, 10, 60

PICTURE CREDITS

مرجع الصور

Archives Charmet: 116

Bayan Naseer & Zain Jamjoom:
3, 11, 13, 15, 19, 29, 39, 49, 65, 73, 80, 85, 89, 94, 119, 127

Bridgeman Art Library:
18, 32, 43 (left), 45, 51 (left), 61 (left), 76, 91, 98, 101 (left), 102, 108, 116

Centre for Islam and Science: 112

Corbis: 117, 118, 120 (left), 120 (right), 124, 125, 126, 127

Dr Kaveh Farrokh kavehfarrokh.com: 21 (right)

Exotic India: 100, 101 (right)

Fred Jones Jr. Museum of Art, University of Oklama: 61 (left)

Fine Arts Library, Harvard College Library: 58

Gabriel Vandervort, www.ancientresource.com:
4, 31 (top left)

Gerard Degeorge: 76

Getty Images:
48, 61 (right, top and bottom), 80, 89, 97 (right), 99 (left), 121, 123, 129

Googleimages: 38, 59

Holden Buyler: 66

Imagesofasia.com: 86, 104

IRCICA, Istanbul: 24

Islamic Foundation:
2, 3, 5, 7, 9, 12, 31 (bottom right), 31 (top right), 47, 53 (right), 93

iStockimages:
6, 30, 50, 51 (right), 53 (left), 55 (top), 21 (left), 74, 79 (left), 84, 99 (right), 103 (left), 105 (left), 109 (bottom), 109 (top)

Kaynak Kitapligi: 88 (left), 88 (right)

Muslimheritageimages.com:
31 (bottom left), 33, 43 (top right), 55 (bottom), 79 (right)

National Museum of Saudi Arabia: 10

Richard Caton Woodville (1846-1927): 108

Royal Asiatic Society, London: 18, 98

Smithsonian National Museum of Natural History: 10, 41

The British Museum: 77 (bottom)

The David Collection: 35, 56, 67, 77 (top)

The Stapleton Collection:
91, 101 (left), 108

Treasury of the Abbey of Saint-Maurice, Valais, Switzerland: 43 (left)

University of Edinburgh: 51 (left)

Victoria and Albert Museum: 63, 102

Wikipedia:
64, 90, 97 (left), 103 (right), 105 (right), 113 (centre), 113 (left), 113 (right)

World Religions Photo Library: 45

Every effort has been made to trace and acknowledge ownership of the copyright of photographs and illustrations. The publishers offer to rectify any omissions in future editions following notification from the copyright holders.